PUERTO RICAN

YOUTH

EMPLOYMENT

JOSÉ HERNÁNDEZ

PUERTO RICAN YOUTH EMPLOYMENT

JOSÉ HERNÁNDEZ

University of Wisconsin, Milwaukee

Waterfront Press
Maplewood, N.J.

HD
8081
P8
H47
1983

Manufactured in the United States of America.
cloth ISBN: 0-943862-07-8
paper ISBN: 0-943862-08-6
For information, write Waterfront Press, 52 Maple Avenue,
Maplewood, N.J. 07040

Dedicated to
Nilza Cristina,
Shani Cibele
and Xavier,
my children.

ACKNOWLEDGMENTS

This study was made possible by a grant from the Rockefeller Foundation to the Puerto Rican Migration Research Consortium. I wish to thank Ralph K. Davidson, Deputy Director of the Foundation's Social Science program, and Mary M. Kritz, Assistant Director, for their review of the proposal and suggestions regarding the research design. Throughout the project, José Oscar Alers, the Consortium's Secretary, contributed valuable advice and organizational support. Howard Stanton, a co-principal investigator in the Foundation's grant, helped to coordinate this study with the National Survey of Puerto Ricans, which he directed.

The computer tapes of the Survey of Income and Education were obtained through the cooperation of Myriam Torres and Mary Wreford of the National Chicano Project, Survey Research Center, Institute for Social Research, University of Michigan at Ann Arbor.

At the University of Wisconsin, my colleagues Joan Moore and William Vélez made suggestions regarding the development of the research and the interpretation of results; Jim Faulkenberg and George Frescos assisted in the bibliographic search; Robert H. Dudley, Paul Fischer and Donald J. Schaeffer helped solve problems in computer programming; Connie Foote and Debbie Ritchie Kolberg typed preliminary manuscripts, and the Social Science Research Facility provided terminal use for tabulations and the word processing services of Donna Bennett in preparing the final draft.

For providing a critical evaluation of the final manuscript and making recommendations for revision, I am grateful to Lois S. Gray, Associate Dean of the New York State School of Industrial and Labor Relations, Cornell University, and Irving Sivin, Director of the Biometrics Unit of the Center for Biomedical Research, Population Council. Lastly, I wish to thank Kal Wagenheim of Waterfront Press for his encouragement and help in the publication of this book.

To these persons and numerous others who encouraged and helped me, I express my sincere appreciation by cordially saying "Muchas gracias!"

José Hernández

Chicago, Illinois
October, 1983

CONTENTS

TABLES AND FIGURES

INTRODUCTION

This study was motivated by concern for the thousands of Puerto Rican teenagers and young adults in the United States, who face many disadvantages and difficulties in finding and keeping a job and in following a career. In as much as the numerical evidence presented expresses a human experience, it attempts to portray the reality of exclusion from effective participation in the American economy, and the conditions that foster uncertainty and disappointment as part of everyday life. The research was directed toward providing some explanation for the depressed situation of Puerto Rican youth, at least as can be determined by analyzing the social and economic characteristics recorded in public data sources.

In a related effort, the author collaborated with other members and staff of the Puerto Rican Migration Research Consortium, in the completion of a national survey of Puerto Rican youth. The sample and questionnaire were prepared so as to supplement official statistics and examine many aspects of the Puerto Rican situation which are not included in routine data collection. Since Puerto Ricans make up only one percent of the total U.S. population, data on this segment tend to be fragmentary or nonexistent when the entire nation is the unit of study. Certain features of the Puerto Rican experience (for example, migration, language, incomplete schooling and inner-city residence) are not matters affecting the majority of the United States population. Standard information items therefore may omit, distort, or overly condense the details needed to adequately study the Puerto Rican population.

In anticipation of a better data base, this volume was limited to information from public data sources and sought to analyze whatever could be validly obtained from them. The principal data source was the Survey of Income and Education, conducted in 1976 by the U.S. Bureau of the Census, in conjunction with the Office of Education of the Department of Health, Education and Welfare. The original directive from Congress called for estimates of school-age children living in poverty families and of persons having limited English proficiency. Because these purposes necessitated a sample frame much larger than usual for the Current Population Survey, additional information was collected, not ordinarily part of the CPS questionnaire. This included such detailed items as food stamp recipiency, work disabilities, health insurance coverage and reasons for not looking for work. (1)

The combination of a large sample and questions related to poverty made the SIE an important data source for studying Puerto Ricans. Also, the records were made available for public use in the form of computer tapes containing all the data collected, except those items that would permit identification of individual respondents. This enabled the author to organize and tabulate the information as considered appropriate for the study of the Puerto Rican population. The SIE public-use tape had 2,035 records for persons self-designated as "Puerto Rican" in response to the question on ethnic origin or descent. When multiplied by sample weights, the basic characteristics of the file were found consistent with information from other data sources, such as the CPS for other years and the 1970 Census. Insofar as these comparisons can be said to indicate reliability, the SIE records seemed to offer an acceptable data base.

Several types of error have been found in the data sources just mentioned. Incomplete coverage or undercount in the Census enumeration and sampling error in the Surveys mean that a certain segment of the Puerto Rican population is not represented. As yet, the characteristics of the omitted segment have not been clearly determined. (2) Mistakes also take place in the recording and processing of information for the population covered by the Census or a Survey. Several problems of this nature will be discussed. The research could not, however, provide remedies for errors in the data sources. Nevertheless, care was taken to avoid the use of distorted or invalid information.

A limiting factor in tabulating public-use files is the small number of cases resulting from detailed specifications. For example, it may be important to determine the extent of work disability among teenagers not completing high school, living in a central-city area, and unemployed. Although such persons certainly exist, the sample tape may have only a few or no cases for this purpose. It is therefore necessary to aggregate enough cases in the categories of a tabulation, to reach valid conclusions. In a study focused on a limited age group, the need for caution in the tabulation of refined categories was a matter of special concern.

In practice, it was found that valid results could not be obtained for age categories smaller than three years. For many purposes, larger age groups were necessary. After extensive consideration, the range from 14 to 31 years of age was selected for detailed study. This provided for three subcategories of six years each (14-19, 20-25, 26-31) which could be split in turn into the three-year minimum unit. In addition, the progression of categories accorded with major life event and change periods; for example, ages 17-19 approximate the usual high school graduation time. The upper limit was significant for Puerto Ricans, in that persons born at the beginning of the large-scale migration to the United States in 1945 were aged 31 in 1976.

In recent U.S. Government publications on the topic of youth employment, the age range is generally 16 to 24 years. (3) Aside from methodological considerations, the broader definition used in this study was considered appropriate for the population researched. Many Puerto Ricans leave school, seek work or have some seasonal work experience at ages 14 and 15. Delays in schooling and the disruptive nature of migration often mean a longer-than-average period of settling into a work pattern. It is therefore important to consider persons approaching 30 years of age.

Another departure from the usual practice is the use of the term "gender" instead of "sex" when reference is made to men and women. In contemporary English, gender is a more precise label because it has less alternative meanings and unrelated connotations. As will be explained in some detail, the term "sole responsibility for a household" has been used to describe the situation of a "female head of household." The United States, including 50 States and the District of Columbia, is referred to as the "continent," in comparison with the island of Puerto Rico. Puerto Ricans living in the United States are said to be "U.S. Puerto Ricans" as a matter of literary simplicity. Whether in the United States or Puerto Rico, I consider a Puerto Rican to be a Puerto Rican without adjectives implying possession.

The reader will detect a bias favoring Puerto Ricans in this publication. I have not modified any of the figures resulting from computer tabulations or those drawn from published sources. I have endeavored to make the organization and format of illustrations and the accompanying analysis an objective presentation. However, as in any research, the personal background of the researcher influenced in the interpretation of the data. My view is that Puerto Ricans remain colonized and deprived in regard to the nation's economy; stigmatized and discriminated in social terms, and among the least advantaged in the United States system. Comparisons with other groups (not possible in this study, for lack of resources and time) would likely confirm this view and provide measures of distance from the bottom, upward. If conclusions and recommendations seem to "go beyond the evidence," they do so on the basis of experience and the conviction that the story must be told in a Puerto Rican way.

1. PUERTO RICAN YOUTH IN 1976

Puerto Ricans have lived and worked in the United States for more than a century. Large-scale migration to the continent, however, began after World War II ended in 1945. The Survey of Income and Education recorded social and economic information about thirty years later. How the community had changed is an essential topic for studying youth employment. Following a summary, this chapter will present introductory details on population growth, migration patterns and geographic distribution, age and household composition, marriage and family characteristics, language and educational background.

SUMMARY

During the 1970s about half of the U.S. Puerto Ricans were younger than 20 years and those aged 20 to 35 made up almost a quarter of the population. Social life centered on childbirth, schooling, job procurement, marriage, household and family formation. The population grew rapidly and persons born in the United States began to outnumber those born in Puerto Rico. In the late 1960s return migration to Puerto Rico had surpassed the movement of people from Puerto Rico to the United States. The relation subsequently reversed and a renewed migration from island to continent has contributed to population growth. Recent migrants from Puerto Rico have been more often women than men, and predominantly 20 to 30 years of age. This has strengthened the trend toward increased women's responsibility for households and the youthful character of the Puerto Rican population. In contrast with the pattern before 1970, women and men have been delaying marriage until their mid-twenties; but a high rate of marital break-up by separation and divorce has continued. An increasing percent of children did not live with both parents, or were living with relatives, and becoming independent early in life. The proportion of young adults who remained a member of their parents' household was also greater. This meant that living arrangements varied considerably and differed from conventional household patterns in the United States.

While families of three to five persons remained typical in 1976, households having one or two individuals had become common—a change related to the marriage and family patterns just mentioned. More than half of the nation's Puerto Rican households were still located in New York City. However, the rate of household formation was higher in other places. Migrants from Puerto Rico had an increased tendency to live in New Jersey, New England, and the North Central States. Puerto Ricans moving within the United States generally moved away from New York City. But regardless of region almost all Puerto Ricans were living in metropolitan areas and most lived in central-city neighborhoods, where the barrios or ethnic communities were located.

Changes in the composition, life patterns and location of the U.S. Puerto Rican population have given the barrios a social character that derives partly from tradition, but results primarily from a need to survive in an alien environment. Behind the numbers on migration, inner-city concentration, women heading households and children living in a segmented world are the harsh realities of an uprooted and poorly transplated people. From this experience, a national society is emerging with a coherence relative to its deprivation and likelihood of continuance as a distinct population.

POPULATION GROWTH

Considerable evidence shows that the U.S. Puerto Rican population has increased during the past ten years. But changes in the definition for designating persons as "Puerto Rican"; incomplete coverage; variation in method; and errors in data collection make it difficult to estimate total numbers and measure population growth in a precisely reliable way. In 1978 the Current Population Survey produced an estimate of 1,850,000 Puerto Ricans or 200,000 more than the SIE estimate of 1,650,000 in 1976, which was about 200,000 more than the 1,450,000 figure from the 1970 Census. (4)

The progression suggests a somewhat accelerated growth rate, the combined result of the reproduction pattern typical of a very young population and increased migration from Puerto Rico.

By 1976 U.S. born Puerto Ricans were about as numerous as those born in Puerto Rico and most were children and teenagers. For lack of birth register statistics comparable with population estimates, fertility rates cannot be currently estimated, except by an elaborate method beyond the scope of this study. It seems reasonable to suppose, however, that an increased proportion of persons reaching the childbearing stage of the life cycle results in a higher reproduction rate for most populations. If this happens among Puerto Ricans and the third and successive generations continue to identify themselves as Puerto Rican, a considerable population expansion will take place. Although a mere speculation at present, the U.S. Puerto Rican population could surpass Puerto Rico's population around year 2000.

The SIE questionnaire included an item on date of entry for persons born outside the United States. Our tabulations showed that an estimated 111,000 adults born in Puerto Rico had moved to the United States from 1970 to early 1976. As shown in Figure 1, this total was greater than the numbers for 1960-64 and 1965-69, periods when migration from Puerto Rico is said to have declined. The difference is not great and may only indicate a continued movement from Puerto Rico at a moderate level. But even a low level of net migration would have contributed importantly to population growth, in that the persons added tended to be young adults, likely to become parents of children born in the United States. (5)

The most convincing evidence of rapid population growth--actual and potential--is the rate of household formation among Puerto Ricans. From 1970 to 1976, households increased from 370,940 to 501,400, a 35 percent expansion or proportionally twice the growth rate of the Puerto Rican population itself. Many of the new households were established by young adults making living arrangements separate from the parent generation and likely to become parents themselves. In any case, more income than previously earned was required for such expansion--which made youth employment a crucial matter for a population in transition.

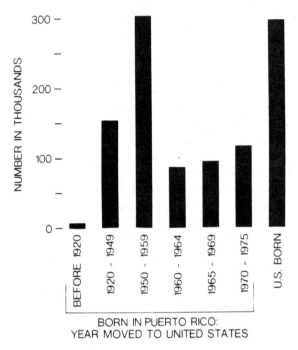

1. PUERTO RICANS IN THE UNITED STATES,
AGE 14 AND OLDER, 1976. NATIVITY AND YEAR MOVED TO U.S.

BORN IN PUERTO RICO:
YEAR MOVED TO UNITED STATES

HOUSEHOLD COMPOSITION

In 1976 Puerto Rican households had an average (mean number) of 3.1 persons, lower than the 1970 average of 3.6, and evidence for a general reduction in the number of members per household. Table 2 shows that the trend involved primarily one-person households, which had previously been the least represented category, and two-person households, which also increased at a much higher rate than all households. There was a decline in households with five or more members--suggesting a diminishing of the "extended" households having relatives and friends in addition to the nuclear family, or a large number of children. The proportion of three and four member households, typical of nuclear families, remained about the same.

2. PUERTO RICAN HOUSEHOLDS IN THE UNITED STATES: PERCENT DISTRIBUTION AND CHANGE RATES BY NUMBER OF MEMBERS: 1970, 1976.

MEMBERS	PERCENT DISTRIBUTION			CHANGE RATE,
	1970	1976	difference	1970-76*
1	11	18	+ 7	121
2	18	21	+ 3	58
3	20	18	− 2	22
4	19	19	0	35
5	14	12	− 2	16
6 +	18	12	− 6	10
ALL	100	100	0	35

*Number of households gained or lost as a percentage of the total in 1970.

Another indicator of these changes is the number of nonfamily households, which more than doubled from 1970 to 1976 and sharply increased from 11 to 20 percent of all Puerto Rican households. A trend away from family households is consistent with changes occurring in the total United States population and the prevalence of young adults among Puerto Ricans. It also reflected a greater tendency toward individual migration, and a departure from traditions stressing family life. During the 1970s, Puerto Ricans were often changing their place of residence and in many cases formed living arrangements alone, with relatives or unrelated persons.

Increases occurred in the number of households with more than one family--those having a "subfamily" with persons related to the household head, or a "secondary" family, involving persons related to one another, but not to the household head. All together, multiple family units numbered 29,214 or 6 percent of Puerto Rican households in 1976. Comparable data were not found in 1970 census publications, but information for 1960 showed that only 4 percent of Puerto Rican households had more than one family. Moreover, subfamilies and secondary families increased three times during the sixteen year period, a higher rate of expansion than household formation, in general. Secondary families increased from 1,299 in 1960 to 10,576 in 1976, more rapidly than subfamilies. Since secondary families are not related to the household head, this change suggests innovative living arrangements, rather than traditional family life. Considering the economic problems affecting Puerto Ricans in the 1970s, both subfamilies and secondary families may also suggest a survival strategy for persons with limited income and employment possibilities.

WOMEN'S ROLE IN HOUSEHOLDS

Until the 1980 Census, official data sources in the United States defined a "head of household" as the adult male regarded as head by the household members and accordingly recorded first in the questionnaire. Only when such a person did not live in a household was a woman considered the head, regardless of the marital or family relations among household members. Thus almost all women recorded as household heads had sole responsibility for their households, in contrast with the shared responsibility typical of male-headed households, which were predominantly husband-wife living arrangements. In recognition of this difference, this study will use the term "women with sole responsibility for a household," instead of "female head of household."

As a percent of U.S. Puerto Rican households, those having women with sole responsibility increased from 15.3 in 1960, to 26.5 in 1970, to 37.6 in 1976, to 41.0 in 1978--the most clearly defined and perhaps most influential trend of community change. (6) If this trend continued, the 1980 Census was likely to record a figure near 45 percent and about half of Puerto Rican households will have a woman as the sole responsible person about 1985. Since a transition of this magnitude has important implications for youth employment, it will be considered in some detail.

Data presented in Figure 3 show that Puerto Rican women of all adult ages have participated in the household responsibility trend, as measured in 1960, 1970 and 1976. Nevertheless, significant differences in the age pattern at each of these dates suggest a succession of change initiated by middle-aged women and adopted in turn by younger age groups. In 1960 the household responsibility rates stabilized in the 20-30 percent range beyond age 40, following on a moderate upward tendency that appears about average for the increasing termination of marriage, as women advance in age. This pattern recurred among women aged 25 to

3. PUERTO RICAN WOMEN IN THE UNITED STATES, 1960, 1970, 1976: PERCENT HAVING SOLE RESPONSIBILITY FOR THEIR HOUSEHOLDS, BY AGE.

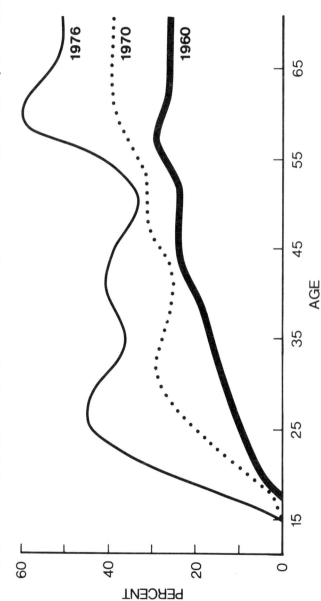

SOURCE: TABULATIONS OF PUBLIC USE TAPES, 15 AND 5 PERCENT STATE FILES OF THE 1960 CENSUS; 20 PERCENT STATE FILE OF THE 1970 CENSUS AND THE 1976 SURVEY OF INCOME EDUCATION.

35 in 1970. In 1976 women aged 20 to 29 showed the most decisive tendency to change toward sole household responsibility--more than 40 percent and very impressive, considering this age group's traditional involvement in a husband-wife living arrangement. Moreover, if the age advancement of the trend-setting groups is considered, an even greater tendency toward sole responsibility is found. Women aged 40 to 50 years in 1960 continued assuming greater responsibility, reaching an unusually high rate when aged 56 to 66 in 1976. A similar progression occurred among women approaching age 30 in 1970, who were in their mid-to-late thirties in 1976, and experienced an increase in household responsibility of more than ten percent during the six year period.

MARITAL STATUS CHANGES

There are, of course, many social factors involved in the trend just described, some unknown for lack of research on the topic. Since marital status is closely related to household responsibility, comparisons of this variable over a several year period serve to raise basic questions. Figure 4 presents a summary illustration of the principal changes taking place from 1960 to 1976. First, a trend toward delaying marriage is evident in the proportions remaining single among teenage and young adult women. The percent married with husband present declined in every age group younger than 45, but the nature of the alternative statuses varied. Separation from husbands was more typical of women aged 25 to 34, combined with an increasing tendency to remain divorced—which explains the unusually high rate of household responsibility at this life cycle stage. The increasing percentages remaining divorced after age 35 suggest a high divorce rate among U.S. Puerto Ricans. It may approach or surpass the divorce rate in Puerto Rico, which resembles that of the United States total population, and is one of world's highest. Divorce has also been said to be a motivating factor in migration from Puerto Rico, for reasons not yet determined in full detail. (7)

Since separation was the principal alternative to a continued husband- wife relation among young adults in 1976, certain aspects of this marital status were examined. First, a small portion of the increase in the separated category may be attributed to a greater

4. PUERTO RICAN WOMEN IN THE UNITED STATES, 1960, 1970, 1976:
PERCENTAGE OF TOTALS BY AGE GROUP, ACCORDING TO
SELECTED MARITAL STATUS CATEGORIES.

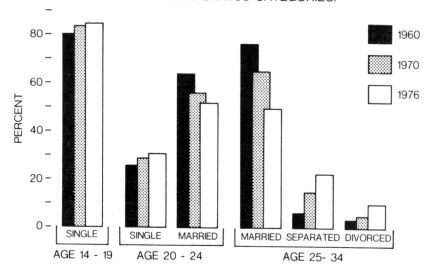

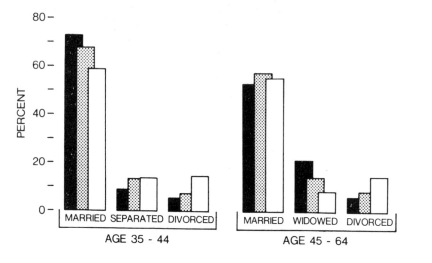

willingness to be so designated. From 1960 to 1976 the percentage reporting an alternative status, "now married, spouse absent" declined from four to less than one percent of women aged 14 to 44. But the principal factor may be the combined result of poverty and the break with tradition evident in data already discussed. Assuming a young woman cannot afford the costs of a divorce and has no immediate plan for remarriage, using her limited resources for other purposes may make sense, especially if the chances of receiving alimony and/or child support are limited or nonexistent. As evidence for this interpretation, the proportion of Puerto Rican women who actually received such payments was less than 10 percent in 1976; that is, regardless of eligibility basis--ever married, separated, or currently divorced. Also, the percentages of separated Puerto Rican women who were not legally separated were high: ages 14-19: 90, ages 20-24: 80, and ages 25-34: 83. This indicates that legal separation (about as expensive as a divorce) had not been obtained and generally could not be claimed as proof of abandonment.

The interpretation just presented differs from the meaning often given to separation among young adult minority women; namely, that separation is claimed as a means of obtaining welfare. This idea finds an easy rationale in the undercount of young adult males, assuming that most men not counted were evading the Census or a survey, to remain invisible for welfare purposes. Some of this may exist, but available information suggests that this explanation has been exaggerated in the case of Puerto Ricans. The number of males reporting separation were about one third of the female total, and practically none were younger than 25 in 1976. Even if a large undercount estimate is added for males age 14 to 31, the total approaches only half of the separated females in this age group. Migration trends to be described may better explain the disparity and further qualify the "disappearing young man" hypothesis. More women than men move from Puerto Rico to the United States, and this includes many separated from their husbands. Although a matter of speculation at present, it seems reasonable that more young men separated in the United States return to Puerto Rico than separated young women.

FAMILY LIFE CHANGES

Further research is also needed regarding the consequences of marital changes and single parenthood for Puerto Rican children and teenagers. The 1970 Census made it clear that many Puerto Ricans younger than 18 years were not being raised in conventional families; only 65 percent lived with both parents, 58 percent if consideration is limited to children born in Puerto Rico. Most of the other children were living with their mother as sole responsible person, but about 5 percent were living with neither parent; that is, they were living with relatives and friends, or had themselves assumed the role of household head. This was estimated from the tabulation on families with "own" children by the number of children in a family; that is, the natural, adopted or stepchildren of the household head. A comparison of these data with the number of persons enumerated by age showed that some 30,000 persons younger than 18 years were not classified as "own" children.

Information from the SIE provided more details relating family composition to youth employment. First, the proportion of children not living with their parents increased sharply in relation to the age of children. Among children younger than 14 years, only 3 percent lived with neither parent; that is, with relatives and friends. By Census definition, only persons aged 14 and older can be classified as head of household. Table 5 shows that the proportion living with neither parent doubled among Puerto Ricans aged 14 to 16. A more dramatic change was evident in the 17 to 19 age group, in which 20 percent were heads of household and only 69 percent lived with either or both parents. This indicates that for certain teenagers separation from the family of origin began before the usual time for high school graduation, or that family circumstances required them to assume responsibility for the hosueholds in which they lived. In either case, a need for employment is evident, as the persons involved were no longer dependent on their parents.

Did early independence among certain teenagers indicate a general weakening of family ties? The data do not support such an interpretation. On the contrary, a significant percentage of Puerto Rican young adults remained living with either or both parents—up to age 29, when family separation seemed complete. The difference between these households and those in which the child assumed responsibility as head may be a matter of chance, depen-

5. PUERTO RICAN YOUTH IN THE UNITED STATES, 1976: HOUSEHOLD RELATION AND MARITAL STATUS BY AGE, GENDER AND MIGRATION BACKGROUND

| | | HOUSEHOLD RELATION: PERCENT | | | | MARITAL STATUS | | |
		"head or wife"	child	other relative	non family	never married	married	seperated divorced widowed
ALL, AGES:								
14-16	100.0	0.6	93.0	5.0	1.4	99.1	0.7	0.2
17-19	100.0	20.9	68.8	6.7	3.6	81.8	12.5	5.7
20-22	100.0	51.2	26.1	3.0	19.7	47.9	43.0	9.0
23-25	100.0	72.9	11.2	4.8	11.2	27.9	53.6	18.5
26-28	100.0	73.2	16.1	0.0	10.7	15.1	51.0	34.0
29-31	100.0	91.3	0.0	0.1	8.6	11.8	65.5	22.7
AGE 14-19:								
men		0.6	88.7	8.8	1.9	99.2	0.8	0.0
women		16.8	79.0	2.5	1.8	84.9	10.2	4.9
AGE 20-25:								
men		44.9	27.6	5.3	22.2	45.2	45.8	9.0
women		75.3	12.1	2.4	10.2	33.7	49.3	17.0
AGE 26-31:								
men		67.5	16.9	0.0	15.6	18.6	68.1	13.4
women		91.0	2.7	0.1	6.2	10.4	52.9	36.7
AGE 14-19:								
U.S. native		7.0	85.1	6.2	1.7	94.0	3.7	2.4
migrated:								
before 1970		12.4	82.8	3.1	1.7	89.0	8.5	2.5
1970-76		28.5	65.0	3.3	3.3	69.9	23.8	6.3
AGE 20-25:								
U.S. native		44.0	32.5	6.1	17.5	52.0	38.0	10.1
migrated:								
before 1970		78.5	14.2	1.0	6.3	21.8	59.9	18.4
1970-76		63.5	7.0	3.8	25.8	41.8	46.8	11.4
AGE 26-31:								
U.S. native		56.2	22.6	0.3	20.9	20.3	44.8	34.9
migrated:								
before 1970		90.4	5.2	0.0	4.9	10.3	61.9	27.9
1970-76		83.7	0.0	0.0	16.3	18.5	60.8	20.7

ding on who was designated as the reference person in the questionnaire. In either case, many young adults lived with their family of origin. Among Puerto Ricans aged 40 and older, labor force participation has been declining and lower than average for the United States, since 1960. This suggests that young adults continuing in their parents' household were likely providers for the family group--a sign of strength in the uprooting circumstances of migration, and a strategy for coping with poverty.

Young men were more likely than young women to remain living with their family of origin. The difference seemed partly a result of a greater tendency among men to remain single. However, beyond age 20 the proportion of women who were separated, divorced and widowed sharply increased, reducing the percentage remaining married to about the same level as among men of the same age. Apparently, young women did not generally return to their family of origin after a marital break-up; or if they did, they were more often classified as household heads, than young men who had never married. The difference also resulted from a greater tendency for young women to migrate from Puerto Rico to the United States, leaving their family of origin in the island. In any case, continued family involvement for young men seemed greater than social expectations would demand, and was more frequent than a nonfamily living arrangement, typically a household shared with a roommate or partner.

It could be argued that continued family involvement was a matter of tradition, deriving from stronger family ties in Puerto Rico, than is generally found in the United States. The data on migration background in Table 5 provide evidence contrary to this idea. Young adults born in the United States continued living with their parents to a greater extent than those born in Puerto Rico. Therefore, exposure to the continental life style of independence from the family of origin did not seem as strong an influence for change as could be expected. This was particularly apparent in comparison with young adults who had migrated before 1970, most of whom moved with the family of origin and began living in the United States while still a child. Persons showing the most detachment from family living arrangements were those who had migrated to the United States in the 1970s. While this seems reasonable for recent migrants, it may represent a temporary situation—to be followed by renewed family strength, if the generational pattern just described continues into the future.

In contrast with the strength of family ties with parents, involvement in marriage was relatively limited among Puerto Rican teenagers and young adults. Although this trend has been described in some detail, the data on migration background clarify an additional aspect. Recent migrants were generally the most involved in a current marriage, followed by persons who had migrated before 1970, and the least involved were those born in the United States. This suggests that exposure to the continental society may influence in the postponement of marriage and preference for a life style different from the traditional husband-wife relation during young adulthood.

A departure from long-term involvement in motherhood was also evident in the SIE data for young women. One quarter of women aged 17 to 49 were not living with children in 1976—by most criteria a high proportion—and less than 20 percent were living with both pre-school and school-age children, which indicates the traditional, high fertility pattern. The 22 percent living with pre-school children only were clearly clustered in age between 18 and 25, suggesting a shortened period of child-bearing. Women living with children aged 6 to 17 made up only 35 percent and were most represented between ages 30 and 45, in succession to younger women with pre-school children. Less involvement in reproduction and an earlier transition from the child-bearing to the child-rearing stage of motherhood has increasingly signified a greater labor force participation and work commitment for women in the United States and similar nations. However, information later presented suggests that life-cycle changes among Puerto Rican young women have not been associated with this pattern.

GEOGRAPHIC DISTRIBUTION

The 1960 Census reported that 74 percent of Puerto Rican households were located in New York State, 73 percent in the New York "Standard Metropolitan Statistical Area" or SMSA. Ten years later the percent had declined to 66 and by 1976 only 56 percent of Puerto Rican households were located in New York State. (8) Data presented for the 1970s in Table 6 show that the household growth rate in New York was about half of the national average, whereas other states had much higher rates. This means that Puerto Rican communities outside New York were growing much faster

6. PUERTO RICAN HOUSEHOLDS IN THE UNITED STATES: GEOGRAPHIC DISTRIBUTION AND GROWTH RATES, 1970-1976.

STATE	PERCENT OF U.S. TOTAL 1970	1976	GROWTH RATE 1970-76	RANK ORDER 1976	PRINCIPAL METROPOLITAN AREAS
New York	66	56	17.2	1	New York
New Jersey	9	11	60.8	2	Newark, Jersey City, Patterson-Passaic
Illinois	6	7	56.6	3	Chicago
Pennsylvania	3	6	173.4	4	Philadelphia
California	4	5	73.6	5	Los Angeles, San Francisco
Connecticut	3	4	76.0	6	Bridgeport, New Haven, Hartford
Massachusetts	2	3	106.3	7	Boston
Florida	2	2	64.1	8	Miami
Ohio	1	2	72.7	9	Cleveland, Lorain
All others*	4	4	72.4		
United States	100	100	37.3		

*States with less than 1 percent of Puerto Rican households in 1970. Ranked just below Ohio in 1976 were Texas, Indiana, Hawaii, Michigan, and Wisconsin. Because of sampling error in these instances, the ranking may not be accurate.

and likely to eventually surpass it in the total number of households. No individual metropolitan area was a close rival to New York City, however. Chicago had the second largest community but only 7 percent of Puerto Rican households, and Philadelphia, with 5 percent, was next in rank.

Almost all Puerto Ricans—regardless of region in the United States— lived in metropolitan areas, typically in the nation's most populated cities. Since 1960 about two-thirds of the total U.S. population has lived in metropolitan areas. Contrary to the majority pattern of residence within metropolitan areas, most Puerto Ricans have lived in the "central city," which means the geographic limits of the political unit with the largest population, generally the core municipality. Table 7 shows that the percentage of Puerto Ricans located in the metropolitan core has been more than twice that of the total U.S. population since 1960. Only a small proportion of Puerto Ricans (at most, one quarter in 1970) lived in the

7. PUERTO RICAN AND TOTAL UNITED STATES POPULATION: PERCENT BY METROPOLITAN RESIDENCE, 1960, 1970, 1976

	PUERTO RICANS			TOTAL POPULATION		
	1960	1970	1976	1960	1970	1976
TOTAL	100	100	100	100	100	100
metropolitan	95	94	97	67	69	67
central city	77	70	83	33	32	28
balance	18	24	14	33	37	39
nonmetropolitan	5	6	3	33	31	33

Source: U.S. Census Bureau. 1960 and 1970 Census. Reports on Puerto Ricans. Statistical Abstract, 1978. SIE tabulations.

metropolitan balance, made up of secondary and satellite cities and suburban townships.

The data suggest that from 1960 to 1970 Puerto Ricans were slightly involved in the general suburbanization trend in the United States. But from 1970 to 1976 this small movement may have reversed, as the percentage in the metropolitan balance sharply declined to its lowest level in the period considered. It is unclear whether the 1976 figures for Puerto Ricans were affected by the sampling procedure used in the Survey of Income and Education. Perhaps households located in central-city areas had a greater probability of being selected and therefore would be more represented in the survey. On the other hand, other major aspects of the Puerto Ricans sampled in the SIE were consistent with Census and Current Population Survey results. In fact, the 1977 CPS showed that 77 percent of Puerto Rican families were located in the central cities of metropolitan areas, about midway between the 70 percent recorded in the 1970 Census and the 83 percent resulting from the SIE. Thus the 1976 figures may somewhat exaggerate the inner-city concentration, but not to the extent of ignoring a suburbanization movement.

The continuity and growth of Puerto Rican barrios in the central city areas of large cities results from three main factors: an increased tendency among migrants from Puerto Rico to move to metropolitan areas other than New York City; the movement away from New York within the United States, and the younger age composition of the Puerto Rican population outside New York—all of which mean a frequent expansion in the number of households. At present, there are no clear signs of change in these factors, nor evidence of a decline in the discriminatory practices that restrict housing availability to certain neighborhoods.

MIGRATION PATTERNS

Responses to the SIE question on year of first entry to the United States (Figure 8) showed that most persons born in Puerto Rico who moved to the United States before the large-scale migration of the 1950s were living in New York City in 1976. The proportion remaining in New York decreased slightly among persons migrating from 1950 to 1964. New York residence was much lower for more

8. PERSONS BORN IN PUERTO RICO: PERCENT BY METROPOLITAN CATEGORY OF RESIDENCE IN 1976, ACCORDING TO PERIOD OF FIRST ENTRY TO THE UNITED STATES.

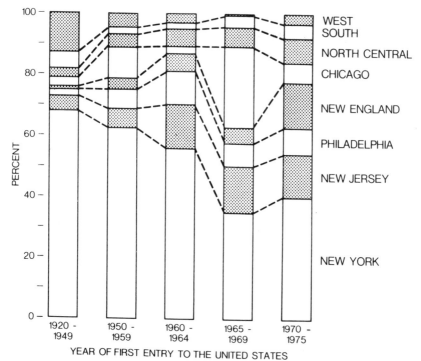

recent migrants from Puerto Rico, only 35 percent among those entering in the late 1960s, when the New York economy was declining and employment opportunities were significantly reduced. (9) Migrants from Puerto Rico during the 1970-75 period had only a slightly greater preference for New York, but more than 60 percent went to live elsewhere. Residential changes occurred between the date of first entry and 1976, and must be considered in the interpretation of these data. However, the entry figures provide a general picture of historical differences in the regional directions of migration from Puerto Rico, adding detail to the basic trend of shift toward places other than New York City.

Outside New York City, the New Jersey metropolitan areas received a consistently large percentage of migrants from Puerto Rico. Migrants in the 1970s showed a somewhat greater movement (about 15 percent) toward New England. This provides evidence for the rapid growth of the Puerto Rican communities in Boston, Hartford, New Haven, Bridgeport, and other cities in this region. More than a quarter of the Puerto Ricans who moved to the continent in the late 1960s remained living in Chicago in 1976. But residence in Chicago declined sharply among migrants entering in the 1970s. Less than 10 percent of the most recent migrants lived in Chicago, about the same number as moved to Philadelphia. Comparing the figures for the 1950s with more recent periods, the aggregate categories defined in Table 9-North Central, South and West-generally gained a slightly greater share of migrants from Puerto Rico.

The SIE included a question on length of residence in the State where the respondents lived. It could be answered "always lived here," or by specifying the number of years. For persons not responding "always lived here," the follow-up was: "In what State (or U.S. territory, foreign country) did you live just before moving to this State?" The results provide measures of stability and migration, especially indicative of movement within the United States. Table 9 shows that in all metropolitan areas, slightly more than half of the Puerto Ricans interviewed claimed to have always lived in their place of residence. This is a higher percentage than were recorded as born in their State of residence, and suggests that the question measured the strength of identification with the place of residence, rather than a precise lifetime migration history. New York, Philadelphia and Chicago, cities with long-standing Puerto Rican communities, had stability rates above the national average.

9. PUERTO RICANS IN THE UNITED STATES, 1976: INDICATORS OF STABILITY AND MIGRATION, BY CATEGORIES OF METROPOLITAN RESIDENCE.

METROPOLITAN CATEGORY*	PERCENT "ALWAYS LIVED HERE"	MIGRANTS: PERCENT HAVING PREVIOUS RESIDENCE IN				
		Puerto Rico	New York City	Next Highest Category		Other Places
New York City	54.8	93.6	—	2.0	Illinois	4.4
New Jersey	47.5	47.9	35.5	4.2	New England	12.4
Philadelphia	52.4	63.3	23.1	4.1	New Jersey	9.5
New England	49.9	62.3	29.3	3.5	New Jersey	9.6
Chicago	58.4	73.1	12.4	4.9	New Jersey	9.6
North Central	46.2	67.5	12.1	8.2	Illinois	12.2
South	36.8	40.2	32.0	16.0	Outside U.S.	11.8
West	42.5	14.4	40.4	11.6	Hawaii	33.6
Total Metropolitan	51.6	74.1	12.5	1.9	Illinois	11.5

*New York includes the New York and Nassau-Suffolk SMSAs. Buffalo, Rochester, and other New York State SMSAs were added to the North Central category, as were the balance of Pennsylvania cities. Otherwise, SMSAs were classified according to the U.S. Census Bureau's major regional designations. For tabulating data on previous residence, Hawaii was considered separately from the West category.

In contrast, places said to be currently attracting Puerto Ricans had lower percentages, especially States in the South category, which includes Texas, Virginia, Maryland, and Washington, D.C.

In Puerto Rican migration, New York City plays a unique role that can be likened to a revolving door. No other metropolitan area has resembled New York in its attractiveness to migrants from Puerto Rico, nor its outward function as a source of migration within the United States. Almost all Puerto Ricans in New York who reported a previous residence specified Puerto Rico, and among all Puerto Ricans specifying the island as their previous residence, nearly 70 percent currently lived in New York—more than would be expected, based on the geographical distribution of the Puerto Rican population in the United States. Apart from Puerto Rico itself, New York City was the principal place of previous residence of migrants living in other metropolitan areas in 1976. This shows how strong New York's gateway relation has been to the rest of the United States, as a source of Puerto Rican migration. For example, in the New Jersey metropolitan areas the number of Puerto Ricans specifying New York City as a previous residence approximated the number from Puerto Rico. This instance also confirms the so-called "spill-over" assertion that many Puerto Ricans living in cities near New York once lived in that city. To a lesser extent, the spill-over pattern seemed true of Philadelphia and the New England metropolitan areas. In the West metropolitan areas, New York City actually exceeded Puerto Rico as a previous residence, suggesting that Puerto Ricans from New York have participated in the same large-scale migration patterns as other United States groups, exemplified by the Northeast-to-Sunbelt-and-West-Coast movement.

Aspects that reflect the history of Puerto Rican migration include the importance of Hawaii as a previous residence of persons living in West Coast cities. Hawaii was one of the earliest destinations for Puerto Rican migration to the United States and in turn became a source of migration to California. (10) A similar sequence has taken place among other ethnic groups migrating to Hawaii, and native Hawaiians, as well. Apart from New York City, Chicago and the North Central metropolitan areas had the highest percentages of migrants specifying Puerto Rico as a place of previous residence. In this region Puerto Rican communities are typically composed of persons born and raised in their city of residence, and those migrating directly from Puerto Rico. (11) In a limited way, Chicago resembles New York City as a "revolving door," or an initial destination for migration from Puerto Rico and a source of subsequent movement in the North Central area. The dispersal of Puerto Ricans in the United States may eventually reduce these regional patterns, but the influence of New York City in the continental migration will likely remain strong.

YOUNG MIGRANTS

Migration has involved almost all Puerto Rican youth, either by personal experience, or as a result of their parents' movement. The direction and volume of migration have varied in time and are reflected in the background of youth, when age is considered. Table 10 shows that in 1976 the percent of Puerto Rican youth who were born in the United States generally declined in the progression from age 8-10 to 29-31. This was as expected, considering the large-scale movement from Puerto Rico of the 1950s, and its subsequent decline. As the migrant population has grown and reproduced, children born in the United States have increased in number. Also, migrants from Puerto Rico have generally been young adults, themselves.

10. PUERTO RICAN YOUTH IN THE UNITED STATES, 1976: MIGRATION BACKGROUND AND LANGUAGE "USUALLY" SPOKEN, BY AGE, GENDER AND NEW YORK RESIDENCE

AGES:	YEAR OF BIRTH	U.S. native	PERCENT ACCORDING TO MIGRATION BACKGROUND — MIGRATED before 1970	1970-75	English only	PERCENT ACCORDING TO LANGUAGE "USUALLY" SPOKEN — English bilingual	Spanish bilingual	Spanish only
8-10	1966-68	85.1	7.5	7.4	12.3	50.6	15.3	21.7
11-13	1963-65	71.2	20.0	8.8	12.1	65.0	14.1	8.8
14-16	1960-62	74.7	20.1	5.1	20.5	58.3	11.9	9.3
17-19	1957-59	69.0	23.6	7.3	7.7	53.2	21.0	18.2
20-22	1954-56	46.2	24.6	29.3	8.6	44.7	23.0	23.7
23-25	1951-53	32.0	44.4	23.6	8.8	45.6	23.9	21.7
26-28	1948-50	27.7	58.4	13.8	9.1	36.4	36.4	18.0
29-31	1945-47	11.4	74.2	14.4	7.0	37.0	33.3	22.8
AGE 14-19:								
men		75.4	21.2	3.4	15.2	59.2	15.3	10.3
women		69.5	22.1	8.4	14.5	53.4	16.4	15.7
AGE 20-25:								
men		49.2	22.9	27.9	14.7	53.1	14.3	18.0
women		31.4	30.4	38.2	3.3	37.8	31.7	27.3
AGE 26-31:								
men		22.8	17.7	59.5	8.5	50.8	32.0	8.8
women		17.4	12.1	70.5	7.8	28.7	36.5	27.1
AGE 14-19:								
New York		81.5	18.5	0.0	16.6	60.2	15.6	7.5
other		62.4	25.1	12.5	12.9	51.6	16.2	19.3
AGE 20-25								
New York		43.5	28.8	27.7	2.4	48.1	25.7	23.9
other		37.0	26.9	36.0	14.1	42.6	21.4	22.0
AGE 26-31:								
New York		24.5	66.6	8.9	6.7	41.1	35.9	16.3
other		13.3	66.4	20.3	9.6	31.5	33.6	25.3

The information on recent migration from Puerto Rico indicated about the same proportion among children and teenagers—less than 10 percent moving from 1970 to 1976. The percentage of recent migrants was three times greater among persons aged 20-22 and continued high among age groups from 23 to 31. This means that a significant proportion of Puerto Rican young adults who lived and sought work in the United States were persons born, raised and educated in Puerto Rico. Table 10 also shows that young women had a much greater percentage of recent migrants than young men, a pattern that has become consistent among Puerto Ricans. Also as expected, the percentage born in the United States was lower in places other than New York City, and the proportion of recent migrants was about 10 percent greater.

The SIE included a question on changes in household composition during the preceding year; that is, whether someone was lost or gained by migration. Tabulations showed that 20 percent of Puerto Rican households were involved in such changes. About 60 percent of these households gained a migrant, which is consistent with the migration/return pattern previously mentioned in regard to the movement between the United States and Puerto Rico. Information on the migrants' characteristics also confirmed the age and gender patterns just described: 40 percent were aged 20 to 25; 68 percent were aged 14 to 31 years old and women outnumbered men.

Only half of the migrants belonged to the immediate family of the household "head," mostly children of the person so designated. The remainder was about evenly divided between "other" relatives (for example, cousins and grandchildren) and nonrelatives; that is, friends and persons sharing the household's living arrangement in some way. About 40 percent of the "other" relatives and nonrelatives were part of a secondary or subfamily; that is, they lived with another person or persons more directly related to themselves than to the household head. Tabulations of households showing a second, third, or fourth migrant indicated that most of the persons gained were children. This suggests that it was relatively common for a migrant to be accompanied by a child or children. The average migrant older than 14 years had no income or received only a few hundred dollars during the year preceding the SIE. About 15 percent received between $2000 and $6000, and 3 percent had a yearly income of $10,000 or more. Except for the last group, the migrants were likely to depend more on the households in which they lived than they contributed toward support.

Another important consequence of migration for Puerto Rican youth was its influence on the language spoken. Since Spanish is the language usually spoken in Puerto Rico and the medium of instruction in public schools, recent migration signifies more people speaking Spanish and literate predominantly in this language. The information in Table 10 on language usually spoken exemplifies this generalization. In 1976 more than half of Puerto Rican children and teenagers usually spoke English, and spoke Spanish as a second language. In comparison, the proportions usually speaking English were lower among young adults, and the percentages usually speaking Spanish were around 45 percent; that is, Spanish only or Spanish with English as a second language. Consistent with the migration patterns described, women were more Spanish speaking than men, as were people living outside New York City, compared with the New York residents. In general, the assumption that by 1976 most Puerto Rican youth were English-speaking was not in evidence. This meant that the average Puerto Rican who sought a job and career advancement was accustomed to speak a language considered "foreign" in the United States, and was likely to speak English with a Spanish accent.

POLICY IMPLICATIONS

Teenagers and young adults (aged 14 to 31) currently make up at least one-third of each major category of the Puerto Rican population—male, female; New York, other. A combined result of reproduction and continued migration from Puerto Rico, youth has become a distinctive feature of this group. Close to 40 percent of the population are younger than 14 years, children who will become teenagers and young adults during the next twenty years. Growing up, attending school, looking for work, making new living arrangements, and trying to get ahead of initial experiences will remain typical of personal and family situations. To be appropriate and effective, the directives, plans and programs intended for Puerto Ricans must be oriented to the needs created by such a condition. The emphasis must be on improving human resources, providing avenues for fulfillment in education and employment, and an environment conducive to career advancement.

In addition, certain characteristics of the population should be considered. Households vary considerably in composition and often differ from the conventional, "nuclear" family pattern. Women have sole responsibility for nearly half of the nation's Puerto Rican households, which implies a heavy burden of providing for children and adolescents. Combining domestic work with employment outside the home requires more effort and greater penalties than average for workers in the American economy. The demands of family care often reduce employment chances to part-time or seasonal jobs. A full-time, yearly commitment to a job outside the home typically involves a high cost that erodes the benefit of additional earnings. In either case, a household's economic situation is weakened. Since there is no sign of change in the trend toward singleparent households, this reality must be dealt with in any effort aimed at improving living conditions among Puerto Ricans.

Contrary to the impressions of the general public, a significant and increasing proportion of the Puerto Rican people live in places other than New York City. Throughout most of the United States, Puerto Ricans are either ignored or considered a small part of a Latino, Hispanic or even "Chicano" category. This partly derives from the fact Puerto Ricans live in the nation's largest metropolitan areas, where their numbers are relatively limited, compared with the rest of the population. Many communities have a large proportion of recent migrants from Puerto Rico or New York City, and are not fully organized to articulate the needs of the average person. Since most individuals are young and inexperienced in community organization, leadership is not readily visible in many instances. The community often includes people with different backgrounds— those raised in the United States, the newly arrived from Puerto Rico, people living close to tradition, as well as those having alternative life styles. The wide variety of social circumstances makes internal unity difficult to achieve and also reduces the effectiveness of whatever participation may take place in the decision-making system. Therefore policy must be sensitive to the dispersal and fragmentation of the Puerto Rican people, and to the frequent lack of correspondence between the stereotype of a Puerto Rican, and reality.

2. HUMAN RESOURCE BACKGROUND

The basic social changes in the Puerto Rican community can be partly attributed to a continuing state of economic depression. If households have unconventional living arrangements, it is mainly because people with limited or no income are seeking ways of survival. The geographic dispersal of Puerto Ricans results from a lack of employment opportunities, both in Puerto Rico and the places where Puerto Ricans live in the United States. Our study of youth employment begins with an overview of household income as a key factor in the community's economic life. This serves to situate the age group researched in the environment which influences their evolution from childhood to maturity, and provides a background for the analytic results to be presented.

INCOME LEVELS AND SOURCES

Figure 11 summarizes annual income data for Puerto Rican households in 1976. At the lowest level, more than 200,000 households received less than $6,000 and about 100,000 households received between $6,000 and $9,000 yearly income. Together, these categories made up 61 percent of all Puerto Rican households, an initial measure of economic disadvantage. Sixty percent of households did not have a savings or checking account, which are possible and useful only when people have more money than "just enough to get by." On the other hand, only 20 percent of Puerto Rican households were owned by the occupants, an attribute indicating one's acceptability for credit and insurance, and receipt of income beyond what is required for basic needs. It seems reasonable to conclude that middle-class status was limited to a relatively small segment of the community, leaving most Puerto Rican households in a condition in which such items as food and rent were major concerns.

The lack of detailed information on the use of income makes it difficult to obtain a more precise measurement of economic deprivation. In U.S. government publications a poverty index adopted in 1969 is used to estimate the number of households having an economic status below a standard of living considered an adequate minimum for the nation's population. The poverty index is updated yearly according to changes in the Consumer Price Index, and ranges in value—depending on "such factors as family size, sex and age of family head, the number of children, and farm-nonfarm residence." Recent information for Puerto Ricans (1978) shows that 39 percent of families were below the "poverty thresholds." This was notably higher than the 31 percent obtained from the SIE tapes, which had 1975 as the reference year for income. (12) Whether the increase represents a significant change cannot be clearly determined because of the limited publication of data on poverty status among Puerto Ricans. For example, the annual Current Population Report series on Spanish origin persons has not provided this information.

An example of the figures used in the calculation of the poverty ratios in Figure 11 was $5500, or the threshold for a nonfarm family of four persons. This amount was somewhat high as an average, since less than half of Puerto Rican households had four or more members and our data included nonfamily households, which would tend to lower the poverty thresholds for the population in general. But for purposes of illustration, 1.5 times $5500 or $8250 can be said to describe the upper reaches of the category just above the poverty line. Together with the categories below the poverty line, this would include about half of the Puerto Rican households. As a social indicator of economic limitations, it makes sense to combine households just above the poverty line with those officially classified as poor. Although a household's income may be somewhat higher than the national minimum standard, particular circumstances such as illnesses or debts may leave little or nothing more than required for basic needs. Two or more earners may be contributing to a family's just-above-poverty status, with individual incomes that rank very low in national comparisons. Puerto Ricans live in high cost-of-living areas and face serious inequities as consumers in housing and retail expenditures.

Experience with Puerto Rican communitites suggests that at least half of the households face serious economic limitations. This becomes more convincing when considering the difference

11. PUERTO RICAN HOUSEHOLD INCOME LEVELS: PERCENT ACCORDING TO DOLLAR AMOUNT RECEIVED AND RATIO OF AMOUNT RECEIVED TO POVERTY "THRESHOLD", DEFINED BY U.S. GOVERNMENT STANDARD INDEX, 1975.

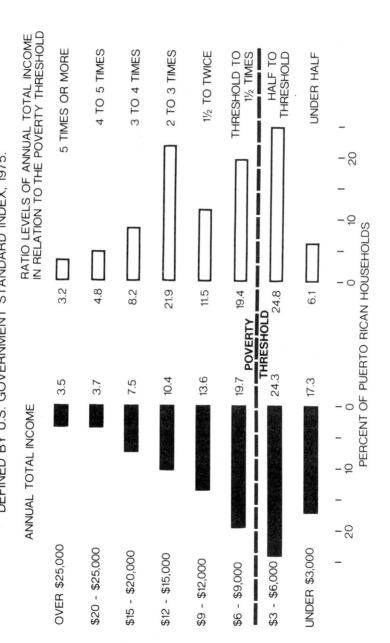

between total household income and amounts received from wages and salaries or "earned" income. According to our tabulations of the SIE files, the mean household income from all sources was $8745 in 1975, but the average from wages and salaries was only $6411, leaving a difference of $2334 from other sources. Among the other sources, only about $400 could be accounted for on the basis of self- employment, farm income, dividends, interest, rentals and royalties. (13) These are receipts in some way related to work or accumulated wealth.

TRANSFER PAYMENTS

The remaining difference of about $1934 was made up of various transfer payments, mainly those associated with the low-income status of Puerto Rican households: foodstamps, aid to dependent children and other welfare payments, unemployment compensation, and subsidized health care payments. Also included were social security, veterans benefits, pensions not directly related to low-income status, but mostly governmental in origin—and small amounts received from other persons in alimony and support payments. Although these income sources are of genuine value to people, their inclusion in household income tends to convey an impression of greater earnings than are received in return for work. If they were considered separately in poverty calculations, the economic condition of Puerto Ricans would look much more depressed than generally portrayed. It would be clear that about one-quarter of the income received by Puerto Ricans is mainly intended to make up for the very low level of income received in payment for work.

It can be argued that transfer payments compensate for people's inability to work and for "structural" factors reducing earned income, such as discrimination and limited job opportunities. According to this view, transfer payments serve to raise the income level of poor people to a minimum living standard and thus provide a solution to poverty. It is further assumed that poor people will find transfer payments an acceptable substitute for earned income. But it also seems reasonable that poor people prefer work for "decent" pay to transfer payments and consider dependence on government programs a negative aspect in their lives. The evidence for either argument remains fragmentary and involves matters going beyond the scope of this book. However, our research produced some related information on eligibility for transfer payments.

Generally speaking, the SIE data on transfer payment receipts showed that Puerto Rican households received less than they were entitled to on the basis of income. For example, an application of eligibility criteria for foodstamps to the income distribution and characteristics of households showed that almost all of those receiving less than the average income of $8735 qualified for participation. (14) Only 32 percent of the households actually received foodstamps, about 15-20 percent less than were eligible. Also, program benefits were limited for households that participated. The mean value of foodstamps was $119 monthly or $1428 annually for Puerto Rican households receiving foodstamps. For this the recipients paid an average of $62 monthly or $744 annually, leaving a net or "bonus" margin of only half of the foodstamp value received. Almost all Puerto Rican households receiving foodstamps received the full allotment and about eighty percent received them for the entire year preceding the survey. Even so, three quarters of the foodstamp households reported spending more than the value of the stamps for food purchases, and 43 percent spent $25 or more monthly in addition to the stamp value—the top category in the questionnaire. Considering that the monthly average stamp value ($119) would buy only part of the food needed by a household of 3 or more persons in 1976, additional expenditures were probably considerably higher than $25 in many cases.

The percentage of households receiving transfer payments from other sources are shown in Table 12. Perhaps the most important finding is that more than half of Puerto Rican households received no transfer payments. Since at least half of the households experienced some kind of economic limitation, it seems reasonable to assume that a margin existed between participation in transfers for income deficiency, and eligibility—as in the case of food stamps. Except for aid to dependent children and other welfare payments, the other sources listed originated from contributions made by the recipients themselves, close relatives or employers. Some of the transfer payments (for example, social security) could be received by affluent people, as well. Thus the participation of Puerto Rican households in transfer payments cannot be precisely equated with economic needs on the basis of the data presented. But the percentages by source provide general evidence for a margin between eligibility and participation, in that higher percentages would be expected on the basis of knowledge from experience with Puerto Rican people in the United States.

12. PUERTO RICAN HOUSEHOLDS AND PERSONS AGE 14 AND OLDER: INCOME RECIPIENCY OTHER THAN WAGES AND SALARIES, ACCORDING TO SOURCE, 1975.

	Percent	
		PERSONS AGE
RECEIVING:	HOUSEHOLDS	14 & OLDER
Aid to Dependent Children	23	11
Other Welfare	8	4
Unemployment/Workmen's Compensation	17	10
Social Security & Other Pensions	17	11
Veteran's Benefits	2	1
None of These	55	75

Note: Percentages are based on individual sources of income and do not total 100 because certain housholds and persons received more than one type of transfer payment.

More specific evidence of a gap between eligibility and participation is provided by the percent of Puerto Ricans receiving aid to dependent children, which was much lower than expected. Among all persons age 14 and older there was a ratio of 1.2 females for every male, and 29 percent of females had sole responsibility for households. Among households headed by women, 61 percent had total incomes below the poverty threshold, and only four percent received alimony or child support payments from private sources. (15) Moreover, only 10 percent of households receiving aid to dependent children received transfer payments from other sources listed in Table 12. This illustrates a general pattern that multiple recipiency of transfer payments was rather limited. Fully 75 percent of Puerto Ricans age 14 and older received no transfer payments and only 13 percent received payments from two or more sources.

The argument presented leads to the conclusion that the economic situation of Puerto Ricans is severely depressed and that dependence on transfer payments is not as great as could be expected in these circumstances. More detailed evidence needs to be examined, to obtain a comprehensive picture. Households must be analyzed in terms of the monetary contributions and eligibility of members, and the characteristics of persons should be studied in relation to transfer payment recipiency. Case histories could document the experience of being poor and a measurement of attitudes would provide information on people's orientation to transfer payments. Nevertheless, our knowledge is now sufficient to say that at least half of the teenagers and young adults who are the topic of this book grew up in an environment of economic deprivation, with little or no recourse for programmatic help or financial assistance. Their schooling, jobs and income have been influenced by the uncertainty and discouragement that are a principal feature of life at the lowest levels of the American economy.

SCHOOLING

The two basic social science approaches to human resource analysis of Puerto Ricans in the United States can be summarized as follows:

1. Most Puerto Ricans have monotonous, humble, uncertain, dead-end and low-paid jobs because the older generation (people who migrated from the island in the 1950s) had limited schooling and fluency in English. Puerto Ricans raised in the United States have the chance to break out of the poverty trap and move up to jobs requiring more education and English proficiency. In time and with sufficient schooling a new generation will obtain creative, prestigious, stable and rewarding employment, and join the mainstream of the American economy and society. (16)

2. Along with blacks, Chicanos, American Indians and other minority groups, Puerto Ricans remain confined to a "secondary" labor market by the racism engrained in American society. Job segregation primarily results from discrimination in hiring and promotion according to social classifications of work as "Puerto Rican" in a way resembling the ascription of nursing and secretarial work to women. Puerto Rican occupations are manual; require little skill or specialized knowledge; demand routine and supervised effort; offer no security or promotion chances, and are paid at the minimum wage level or less. To qualify, one does not need a great deal of formal instruction, and in many cases, reading and writing are not required or of much use. Schooling and "language"

requirements serve as means for exclusion from the desirable, promising and higher-paid jobs in the "primary" labor market. The school system shares these values and behavioral rules, discourages Puerto Ricans from success in formal instruction, and socializes them into resignation to jobs having few advantages. Today's generation of new workers may have somewhat higher educational attainment and English proficiency than their parents, but relative to the rest of society, they are still excluded from jobs ascribed to the middle and upper strata. The few who break out of the poverty trap make up an elite who serve to maintain the myth of opportunity and control the minority group by their "role-model" leadership. (17)

Neither of these perspectives can be proved or disproved on the basis of the data to be presented, because to do so would require much more than is available from the sources of information used. For example, it would be necessary to measure the organization and process of schooling, employment and earning money in the actual situations affecting Puerto Ricans. Opportunity and discrimination would have to be examined as they take place, and the attitudes of Puerto Ricans and the majority group toward school, jobs and income would need to be researched. Ideally, the design would be a longitudinal set of observations, but the elements could be assembled by a variety of methods—case histories, field experiments and survey questionnaires. No study known to the author has yet attempted a comprehensive evaluation of this nature.

During recent years, the typical study reaches conclusions based on an analysis of the aggregate characteristics of Puerto Ricans and observations about the social and economic environment in which they live and work. For example, high school attrition (the drop- or push-out rate) has been shown to be high, relatively unchanging, and related to such factors as being left back in grade; the school attainment and economic status of parents; whether a student lives in a small, recently expanded Puerto Rican community, or in a city having a large and long-standing Hispanic population. The nonattendance rate is said to "indicate" the relative quality of instruction and the school system's roles in assisting students to attain a secondary education. (18) But the link is not measured; the nature of schooling is assumed to be a background factor having some influence on the characteristic measured. So too, the unemployment rate is said to indicate the relative availability of jobs and such factors in employment as discrimination.

Except for descriptive evidence regarding the school system and the labor market, these inferences rely on inter-group and cross-sectional comparisons for validity. If high school nonattendance and unemployment are greater for Puerto Ricans than for majority persons in the same circumstances, something in the social and economic environment is said to disfavor Puerto Ricans. Similarly, if Puerto Ricans with the same background and characteristics have higher nonattendance and unemployment rates in one location as compared with another, a difference in opportunity may exist between these environments. Some social scientists would say that the projective value of these inferences remains tentative, awaiting a direct measurement of environmental conditions and their effect on Puerto Ricans. Until such time as this kind of research is completed, however, most social scientists concerned with Puerto Ricans prefer a provisional analysis to continued ignorance on topics so important to the community's wellbeing.

For example, a timely question finding some answer in the SIE data is whether any change appeared in the school enrollment and attainment of Puerto Rican youth, as compared with previous studies. Table 13 shows that almost everyone aged 14 to 16 was enrolled in school, the same as in 1970. Among students aged 14 to 16, more than a quarter were a year or more behind the usual completion schedule, or "modal" grade for their age—also about the same as in 1970. The usual schedule begins with first grade at age seven and terminates with completion of the twelfth grade at age eighteen. To illustrate, a 14-year-old enrolled in the seventh grade or below is considered delayed in schooling. Among Puerto Ricans aged 17 to 19 in 1976 less than 60 percent were enrolled in school and among those out of school, about 90 percent had not obtained a high school degree. This rate of nonattendance was about the same as in 1970. Previous research found that the delay rate among early teenagers was closely related to nonattendance among those approaching the usual completion of secondary school at age 18. That is, where there was a pattern of frequent "left backs," the "push-out" rate was high; and where Puerto Rican students advanced on schedule, the chances of graduating were better. Since there was no change from 1970 to 1976 in the variables involved, we assume that the general picture of schooling remained about the same. (19)

Because certain persons return to school or continue their education beyond age 18, attainment measures for older age categories are generally considered more predictive of formal preparation for work careers than data for teenagers. Among Puerto Ricans aged 26 to 31 in 1976 about 60 percent had not completed high school. This measure was about the same as found among those aged 19 to 24 in 1970, or approximately the same group of people. The face-value conclusion is that schooling after age 18 was a consistently limiting factor in formal preparation for work. However, Table 13

13A. SCHOOL ENROLLMENT OF PUERTO RICANS AGED 14-31, BY GENDER AND NEW YORK RESIDENCE, 1976.

		NOW ATTENDING: PERCENT IN			
	PERCENT ENROLLED	Delayed Grade*	Elemen-tary	High School	Technical, College
ALL, AGES:					
14-16	95.9	26.7	38.0	62.0	0.0
17-19	58.1	17.3	0.0	66.2	33.8
20-22	24.4	25.5	0.0	35.7	64.3
23-25	13.4	--	0.0	21.8	78.2
26-28	8.4	--	0.0	0.0	100.0
29-31	9.5	--	0.0	0.0	100.0
AGE 14-19:					
men	85.3	29.6	25.7	69.6	4.7
women	73.9	17.8	25.7	57.3	17.0
AGE 20-25:					
men	19.4	46.1	0.0	23.3	76.7
women	19.7	37.6	0.0	40.3	59.7
AGE 26-31:					
men	4.7	--	0.0	0.0	100.0
women	11.4	--	0.0	0.0	100.0
AGE 14-19:					
New York	83.5	15.6	25.1	63.4	11.5
other	74.4	27.3	26.5	63.3	10.2
AGE 20-25:					
New York	21.9	29.1	0.0	38.4	61.6
other	17.6	54.5	0.0	25.8	74.2
AGE 36-31:					
New York	6.7	--	0.0	0.0	100.0
other	11.7	--	0.0	0.0	100.0

*Percent of enrolled students in an age group who are one or more years behind the modal grade for their age.

also shows that the percentage of high school noncompletion was somewhat lower than 60 percent in the 20-22 and 23-25 age categories.

Does this signify a change in the schooling pattern? A closer look reveals that the improvement was more attributable to current enrollment than attendance during the teenage years. Fully one quarter of the Puerto Ricans aged 20 to 22 and 13 percent of those

13B. SCHOOL ATTAINMENT OF PUERTO RICANS AGED 14-31, BY GENDER AND NEW YORK RESIDENCE, 1976.

	NOT ENROLLED: PERCENT WITH			
	Less Than HS Degree	HS Degree	Some Post-Secondary	College Degree
ALL, AGES:				
14-16	100.0	0.0	0.0	0.0
17-19	89.5	10.5	0.0	0.0
20-22	40.5	44.1	15.4	0.0
23-25	43.6	31.7	17.3	7.5
26-28	63.1	27.0	8.2	1.8
29-31	58.0	31.1	8.8	2.1
AGE 14-19:				
men	90.5	9.5	0.0	0.0
women	90.7	9.3	0.0	0.0
AGE 20-25:				
men	38.5	39.0	20.9	1.5
women	45.1	37.7	11.9	5.3
AGE 26-31:				
men	55.1	24.1	17.1	0.8
women	63.9	32.1	3.2	3.7
AGE 14-19:				
New York	90.2	9.8	0.0	0.0
other	91.0	9.0	0.0	0.0
AGE 20-25:				
New York	34.3	39.9	23.1	2.7
other	47.8	37.1	11.0	4.0
AGE 36-31:				
New York	57.6	36.8	5.6	0.0
other	64.3	19.1	12.3	4.4

aged 23 to 25 were attending school, notably higher than comparable measures for 1970. A significant portion were still enrolled in high school—most likely to make up for delays and noncompletion through General Education Degree (GED) and similar programs. The remainder were attending post-secondary specialty schools (called "technical") or colleges and universities. Data limitations made it impossible to determine how many were enrolled in technical schools, as distinct from college. Among persons aged 20 to 25 who were not enrolled about 16 percent had attained some post-secondary schooling—twice the percentage among older persons. This suggests that the change primarily involved technical schooling, although the same category includes individuals with less than four years of college education.

Perhaps the only valid conclusion is that from 1970 to 1976 no significant change occurred in schooling up to age 20, but more persons went back to school in their early twenties than previously found among Puerto Ricans. Because of the potential importance of the return for employment, attention was given to differences in schooling according to the basic characteristics of the population. First, we found that delays in schooling were more frequent among teenage men than women, but men had a greater tendency to stay enrolled in school. The net result was about the same school attainment for men and women up to age 20. About the same proportion of men and women returned to school in their early twenties, but women were more frequently enrolled in technical schools and college and had a higher percentage of college degree attainment. This seemed attributable partly to a background of greater delays among men, and partly to a tendency among women returning to school to have already completed high school. In other words, women who as teenagers had left school before graduation were not typically among those who later returned to school. This means that a somewhat greater disparity in educational background resulted among women; that is, between the many who had less than a high school degree and never returned to school, and those who continued their schooling beyond the secondary level. For men, the return primarily signified a remedial effort for completing high school or learning a technical specialty, assumed to represent an approach to the "middle" level of formal preparation for work.

Puerto Rican teenagers living in New York City tended to stay enrolled in school to a greater extent than those in other places. Previous research had produced the same result and attributed the difference to a policy favoring promotion according to the usual schedule of grade attainment. (20) Data from the SIE (Table 13) provided additional evidence for this relation, but it also showed that up to age 20 the attainment of students who stayed enrolled in school was about the same in or out of New York City. A contrast analogous to that between men and women was found between Puerto Ricans older than 20 living in New York, and those in other places. In New York a higher percentage of persons returning to school were completing high school, and a higher percentage eventually attained a secondary, technical or "middle" level of formal preparation for work. In other places, the return was primarily among persons who had already graduated from high school and the eventual attainment of college degrees was proportionately greater. Again, Puerto Ricans who had left school as teenagers had not returned to school as much in places outside New York and differed more notably in formal preparation for work, compared with persons having advanced schooling in the same communities.

Thus far the research results can be explained by the secondary labor market perspective in that no change was apparent in the general outcome of the established means of preparing people for work. Most Puerto Rican teenagers were still leaving school before graduation, typical of an underclass of workers expected to seek the kind of jobs ascribed by the economy to the lower strata of society. The emerging trend of a return to school was mainly remedial in nature and focused on access to a middle level of preparation for work—jobs above average for the secondary labor market, and open to Puerto Ricans. Segments of the Puerto Rican population facing greater disadvantages than others—women and/or persons living in numerically small communities—tended to not participate in the return to school, except as already over the hurdle of high school graduation. These exceptions illustrate the making of a group who evade the low-paid and dead-end job condition of the average person, but who are nevertheless subject to prejudice and discrimination as Puerto Ricans.

According to the assimilation perspective, the disadvantages of being Puerto Rican should lessen as birth and socialization in the United States result in people who resemble the American majority in their way of life. This idea has motivated educational policies (particularly bilingual programs of the transitional type) to stress the importance of achieving proficiency in the English language.

An initial evaluation of the assimilation perspective can be made on the basis of data presented in Table 14, which address the topic of formal preparation for work in terms of two variables: migration background and language usually spoken by Puerto Rican youth. These measures were earlier described in relation to Table 10, Chapter 1.

The percentages of delayed schooling and enrollment among teenagers provide evidence for the assimilation perspective, particularly in regard to the migration variable. Generally speaking, birth and length of residence in the United States and predominant use of the English language were associated with grade promotion on schedule and continued enrollment in school. However, the information on school attainment suggests an important qualifying aspect. Among teenagers staying enrolled in school, the proportion continuing their education beyond high school varied inversely with the degree of assimilation. In other words, teenagers born in the United States and those usually speaking English had an easier time of graduating from high school, but were less inclined to seek further schooling than the survivors of the school system who had migrated from Puerto Rico and usually spoke Spanish.

The data for persons older than 20 years showed a somewhat different pattern. Puerto Ricans born in the United States and those usually speaking English returned to school in higher proportions than migrants from Puerto Rico and the Spanish-speaking. They also tended to be enrolled in technical schools and college, instead of high school. However, this was not fully indicative of eventual attainment of formal preparation for work. Compared with Puerto Ricans born in Puerto Rico, those born in the United States had a higher percentage of high school graduates and persons with some post-secondary schooling. But recent migrants from Puerto Rico had a higher percentage of college graduates than Puerto Ricans born in the United States. Again, this seems to between indicate that the most assimilated persons stop short of the higher levels of human resource formation. More concretely: if almost half of the Puerto Rican young adults born in the United States graduate from high school, one would expect more than 3-5 percent to graduate from college. Instead, most tend to remain at the middle level previously mentioned as typically preparing an individual for an above-average job and not necessarily for an occupation in the primary labor market. (21)

The higher percentage of college graduates among recent migrants from Puerto Rico suggests an increased number of persons with advanced schooling in the flow of people to the continent. In fact, the general school attainment pattern of recent migrants surpassed that of migrants arriving before 1970, which indicates a greater transfer of human resources at the middle level, as well. An important difference seems to be that recent migrants were predominantly schooled in Puerto Rico, whereas those migrating before 1970 had some, most or all of their school experience in the United States. The data in Table 14 show that for persons born in Puerto Rico, exposure to schooling in the United States had decidedly negative consequences in terms of educational attainment. Less than 30 percent of migrants arriving before 1970 eventually graduated from high school and only a small fraction obtained a college degree.

The patterns just described help explain why there were no college graduates among Puerto Rican youth who spoke only English as their usual language, and why relatively few recent migrants and those speaking only Spanish participated in the return to school. The school attainment of most Puerto Rican young adults (those who were bilingual) was also consistent with the patterns by migration background. Persons predominantly English-speaking were concentrated in the categories of high school graduate and some post-secondary schooling. Those predominantly Spanish-speaking showed a disparity between a large percentage not completing high school and a moderate proportion of college graduates.

In summary, our research provided only marginal evidence in support of the assimilation perspective; namely, that for Puerto Rican children enrolled in the U.S. elementary and secondary school system, being U.S. born and predominantly English-speaking helps in reaching a high school degree. But this does not necessarily mean an eventually higher educational attainment than was found among persons born in Puerto Rico or those predominantly Spanish-speaking. The more assimilated seem less inclined to obtain a college degree, whereas migrants from Puerto Rico who bypass the U.S. elementary and secondary school system are increasingly represented among those at the higher levels of human resources.

These differences provide evidence favoring a secondary labor market perspective. According to this view, assimilated Puerto Ricans are discouraged in their socialization from aspiring to posi-

14A. SCHOOL ENROLLMENT AND ATTAINMENT OF PUERTO RICANS AGED 14-31, BY MIGRATION BACKGROUND, 1976.

MIGRATION BACKGROUND	PERCENT ENROLLED	NOW ATTENDING: PERCENT IN				NOT ENROLLED: PERCENT WITH			
		delayed grade*	elemen-tary	high school	technical, college	less than HS degree	HS degree	some post-secondary	college degree
AGE 14-19:									
U.S. native	81.8	16.9	26.0	65.3	8.7	86.1	13.9	0.0	0.0
migrated:									
before 1970	75.6	40.6	24.3	58.8	16.9	97.7	2.3	0.0	0.0
1970-76	59.9	55.9	27.0	51.2	21.8	100.0	0.0	0.0	0.0
AGE 20-25:									
U.S. native	28.7	37.9	0.0	13.4	86.6	21.6	45.6	29.6	3.2
migrated:									
before 1970	18.4	50.0	0.0	40.8	59.2	52.0	29.8	16.1	2.1
1970-76	7.4	37.7	0.0	0.0	100.0	54.8	39.4	0.6	5.2
AGE 26-31:									
U.S. native	12.2	--	0.0	0.0	100.0	39.7	48.2	7.1	4.9
migrated:									
before 1970	9.4	--	0.0	0.0	100.0	70.1	22.0	7.6	0.4
1970-76	2.5	--	0.0	0.0	100.0	44.6	36.0	14.4	5.1

14B. SCHOOL ENROLLMENT AND ATTAINMENT OF PUERTO RICANS AGED 14-31, BY LANGUAGE(S) USUALLY SPOKEN, 1976.

USUAL LANGUAGE	PERCENT ENROLLED	NOW ATTENDING: PERCENT IN				NOT ENROLLED: PERCENT WITH			
		delayed grade*	elemen- tary	high school	technical, college	less than HS degree	HS degree	some post- secondary	college degree
AGE 14-19:									
English only	88.0	22.7	33.4	66.6	.0	100.0	0.0	0.0	0.0
English, bil.	83.4	17.8	23.1	66.8	10.1	83.6	16.4	0.0	0.0
Spanish, bil.	62.0	56.9	33.0	45.1	22.0	97.9	2.1	0.0	0.0
Spanish only	71.2	19.1	20.7	61.4	18.0	91.9	8.1	0.0	0.0
AGE 20-25:									
English only	23.9	32.4	0.0	0.0	100.0	34.6	46.9	18.5	0.0
English, bil.	23.5	31.9	0.0	26.4	73.6	24.1	44.0	28.8	3.0
Spanish, bil.	19.4	43.2	0.0	37.8	62.2	55.6	27.1	8.3	9.1
Spanish only	11.2	87.1	0.0	0.0	100.0	65.6	32.7	1.7	0.0
AGE 26-31:									
English only	38.0	--	0.0	0.0	100.0	39.7	53.5	6.8	0.0
English, bil.	7.8	--	0.0	0.0	100.0	49.1	27.3	21.2	2.5
Spanish, bil.	8.6	--	0.0	0.0	100.0	73.0	25.3	0.6	1.2
Spanish only	0.5	--	0.0	0.0	100.0	65.1	32.0	0.0	2.6

*Percent of enrolled students in an age group who are one or more years behind the modal grade for their age.

tions beyond the middle level; their career horizons are limited to the more desirable jobs open to long-standing non-European minorities—blacks, Chicanos and American Indians, in particular. The limitations are a normative aspect of an internal colonial organization, based on a differential ascription of social status and economic exploitation by the white majority of European origin.

Insofar as Puerto Rico participates in the same social and economic order, similar developmental limitations affect its human resources. (22) The Commonwealth's policy of favoring universal elementary and secondary schooling does not fully accord with the realities of economic dependency on the United States and its preference for a capital-intensive model for development. So too, the island's drive to facilitate higher education in the 1960s and 1970s was bound to result in a surplus of college-educated people. The recent shift toward more frequent migration of middle-to-higher levels of human resources thus derives from the island's social and economic condition of colonization. In the United States, a Spanish-speaking, bilingual person born and raised in Puerto Rico poses less of a threat to the caste system than someone behaving like the dominant majority, except for being Puerto Rican. An island identity serves to keep alive the myth of Puerto Rican as "foreign" and suits the purpose of social control by developing an intermediary elite between the dominant majority and the mass of poor people struggling to survive on low-paid, dead-end jobs.

CONCLUSIONS

No matter what causal explanation may be proposed for continued poverty among Puerto Ricans, there is general agreement on the consequence for human resource development. Also, the experience of growing up in the limited economic circumstances described is about the same, whether it took place in Puerto Rico, in the United States or in both places. One's survival and that of kin and significant others becomes a fundamental career goal. The strategies include formal education largely because wherever Puerto Ricans are located, elementary schooling is compulsory. Essential aspects of socialization include learning that schooling is mostly unrelated to survival chances; that these chances depend on white, Anglo forces over which Puerto Ricans have little or no control; and that the average person is bound to a life of subordination, dependence, and second-class citizenship. Except for individuals enabled by personal circumstances to seek an exit from poverty in advanced schooling, Puerto Rican teenagers seem to find limited meaning and economic value in completing a secondary school curriculum. They compare "staying in" with such options as migration; learning the normative aspects of making it at the bottom of society; exploring conventional and other ways of earning a living; marriage, military service and similar institutionalized evasions; getting a head start on the jobs open to Puerto Ricans, and investing the time and energy demanded by schooling into finding out how they fit in a world of lifelong uncertainty and very modest aspirations. The common features of these options is a quest for luck (as in the roll of dice in a board game having a series of unrelated episodes with prescribed rewards and penalties) and the realization that formal instruction has little to do with success in the rules and regulations of a "rational" approach to the adult job market.

This differs from the "culture of poverty" perspective in several fundamental ways. (23) Rather than looking at poor Puerto Ricans as locked into an underclass by socialization for failure, the model emerging from our experience views all Puerto Ricans (island and continent) as struggling for success in a field of odds set against them by a superordinate society having a social, economic and political ideology contrary to their best interests. The apathy derives not from a fatalism transmitted through generations, but from a realistic assessment of one's capitivity in a racist order that says "you're not OK" from the cradle onward. The major question should not be why Puerto Ricans continue submerged in poverty, but how they manage to survive and achieve some degree of human advancement in a world of continually negative conditions. We should be asking how the shackles of poverty can be removed by changing the society, instead of how Puerto Ricans can change to suit the society's purposes.

Human resource development models commonly assume a cost-benefit relation between education and employment and a basically "open" society in which upward mobility is not just possible, but primarily a result of individual initiative and achievement. (24) Regardless of variations adapted to societies having a caste system, the evidence presented up to now and many other sources make it apparent that the basic notions cannot be validly applied to Puerto Ricans. (25) In this case a superordinate society imposes certain structural negations of the cost-benefit relations between education and employment, and severely restricts the openness of social mobility. It obliges the subordinate society to seek some alternative to the traditional match between talent and economic activity and (lacking a more sophisticated strategy) to rely on chance as a logical response. For Puerto Ricans, the need for a totally new model of human resource development is strengthened by the economic outlook for island and continent. What is ahead for today's youth is a postindustrial order of scarcities in work in all but those occupations typically open to the affluent and powerful, by social preference. Unless there is a change of path, the average person must be prepared for a lifetime of "hustling" for survival.

3. WORK CAREERS

At the peak of the migration from Puerto Rico to the United States in 1955, an Anglo economist commented that it was "natural" to find most Puerto Rican workers employed in manufacturing, since they had "good manual dexterity," low turnover, and were willing to start at low job levels, "even though they may have higher skills." It was in response to "demands of advancing industry for semi-skilled and unskilled workers (that) Puerto Ricans throughout the country can now be found in mills, factories, mines, shops, and in hundreds of occupations running from miners to assembly workers in electronics, toys, novelties, plastics and food processing." (26) The jobs in which Puerto Rican migrants were typically employed belonged to the "operative" category—routine, repetitive tasks in a factory producing a standardized article for mass-market distribution. This often involved either the grading and sorting of materials, an assembly function, the activiation of a machine, a finishing task, or wrapping and packing the manufactured item in a continuous line of production. Continued employment depended on a worker's endurance and productivity (as evaluated by the checker and supervisor) and on the volume of production—which varied from time to time as a function of market conditions and the company's financial situation. In most cases, there was little or no chance to move up to a permanent position; the workers did not belong to a union, nor could they readily organize to seek improvements on a collective basis. Wages were therefore as low as the level for which the poorest people were willing to work, and fringe benefits were either the minimal legal requirements, or simply did not exist. (27)

Since the 1950s many of the jobs performed by Puerto Rican migrants have been eliminated by the increased trend toward mechanization, automation and (more recently) the computerization of production. Perhaps the most dramatic example is the textile and apparel industry. Technical changes in the machines that comb, dye, spin, twist, knit and weave have made manual activation or control largely unnecessary. Machines now perform the tasks formerly done by cutters, sewers, stichers, ironers and pressers in making clothes. Many companies implementing the modernization of production have closed the plants where Puerto Rican migrants worked, in preference for newly equipped installations in far-away places. Thousands of Puerto Rican workers have been displaced in the process and the needlework category of jobs has sharply declined. (28)

To what extent is the decline in operative work evidenced among Puerto Rican youth today? Is the new generation oriented toward a factory career, or are they performing other types of jobs? Figure 15 was organized to provide a comprehensive and concise answer to this question. A somewhat unorthodox method was used to simplify a very complicated matter. First, technical problems required us to limit the presentation to occupational categories in which a substantial number of Puerto Ricans were recorded as employed in 1960, 1970 and 1976. Data were therefore omitted for managers, sales workers, farmers, and farm laborers, and for women in laborer, professional and craft occupations. Secondly, the absolute numbers of workers were considered a more direct measure of expansion or decline in job markets, than a percentage distribution by employment sector. Lastly, the age categories were not uniformly divided, nor made precisely comparable with those used in other portions of this book. This was partly necessitated by the format of data published for 1960 and 1970, but also reflected the proportional representation of Puerto Ricans by age and the need for comparisons between young and mature workers.

The numerical significance of youth can be appreciated by comparing figures in the various age categories according to the sequence of time. Generally speaking, the numbers of workers aged 20 to 24 approached the numbers aged 25 to 34, and these in turn resembled the totals for workers 35 to 64 years of age. Moreover, very few of the workers younger than 35 in 1976 and almost none of those younger than 25 in 1970 were in the labor force in 1960. Thus a major portion of the workers represented in Figure 15 began their employment during the sixteen year period considered. The main purpose of placing the three dates together in each age category was to determine continuity or change in the jobs performed, with the succession of labor force entry and advancement in age. For example, did teenagers in 1976 do the same or different kinds of work as teenagers in 1970, or teenagers in 1960?

Some ideas can also be gathered about the experience of Puerto Rican workers as they have advanced in age. The correspondence between time periods and age categories was not exact, however. For example, workers aged 14 to 19 in 1960 were 24 to 29 in 1970 and 30 to 35 in 1976, which are only part of the 25-34 age categories. Changes in employment status and mobility from one job category to another were not considered, as well. Nevertheless, a comprehensive view of the historical progression can be obtained by comparing each age group with older groups at later dates.

The most basic finding is that factory work is alive and well among Puerto Ricans. In 1976 the operative category continued having more workers than any other, and included thousands of workers who had entered the labor force after 1960. Continuity was especially apparent among workers aged 35 to 64 in 1976, people who were 19 to 48 in 1960 and primarily represented the migrants of the 1950s. Large numbers of young women were also employed as operatives, especially those 25 to 29 years of age in 1976. Although factory work had declined notably among men aged 25 to 29, it remained the most frequent kind of employment for those in their early twenties.

Regarding 1976, many of the younger workers had entered the labor force subsequent to the decline in the availability of factory jobs. It was therefore important to determine whether a change had occurred in the nature of the operative work performed. Tabulations of the SIE records by specific occupations showed that most Puerto Ricans in 1976 remained in routine assembly line and packaging functions, typical of "light" manufacturing or the production of nondurables. About forty percent of the operatives younger than 35 years were employed either as polishers, sanders, grinders, drillers and lathers (jobs more frequently part of "heavy" manufacturing) or in jobs different from traditional lines of production, such as photographic processing. A few individuals were recorded as checkers or inspectors, positions having a higher social status in a factory than assembly work or packaging. Whether this involved a significant change could not be clearly determined, since published occupational data and studies for 1960 and 1970 did not have this degree of refinement.

An important change evidenced by our data is that operative work is much less frequent among teenage workers, compared with previous times and older workers. By 1976 employment in clerical jobs had notably increased among Puerto Rican young women in general, and was much higher than factory work for those 14 to 19 years of age. In fact, there were more clerical workers than operatives among women younger than 26 in 1976. This meant that many began their work careers in white- or pink-collar positions, of which typist, file clerk, "miscellaneous and not-specified clerical worker" were by far the most typical. Tabulations by specific occupations showed that some women in their twenties worked as bank tellers, cashiers, postal clerks and teachers aides. But relative to the general office helpers, these workers were few and their jobs probably differed only somewhat from the routine, low-paid and dead-end condition of entry-level clerical positions. Thus, the

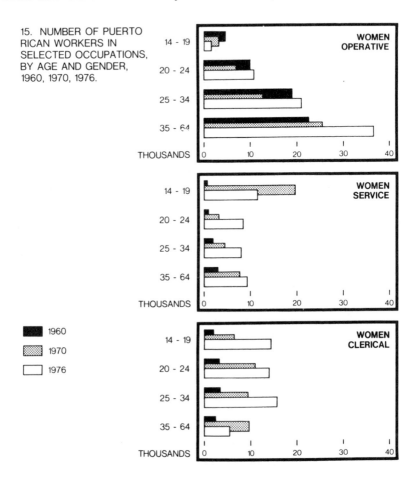

15. NUMBER OF PUERTO RICAN WORKERS IN SELECTED OCCUPATIONS, BY AGE AND GENDER, 1960, 1970, 1976.

historical change involved a transition from the predominance of marginal factory work to similar types of employment in bureaucratic settings.

The same transition was found among Puerto Rican young men, but in the direction of service work as busboys, dishwashers and food service workers, attendants at amusement and recreational facilities, welfare and health aides and orderlies, cleaners and janitors. In this instance, the trend was apparently begun by older workers. In 1960 service work of the type described ranked second to factory operative jobs among men 35 to 64 years of age, and their numbers increased at each subsequent date. Other changes

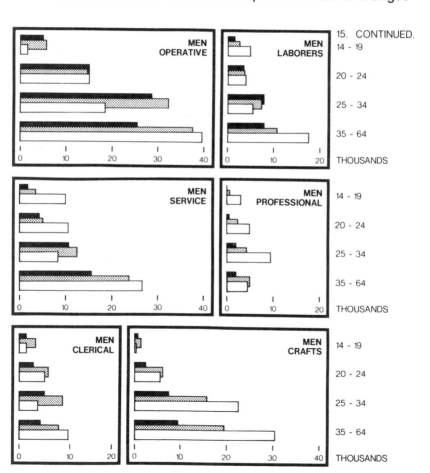

to be presently discussed have more recently altered the job situation of older Puerto Ricans. Nevertheless, youth employment in the 1970s was evidently influenced by the parent generation's involvement in the menial aspects of cleaning, health and food services. From this a stereotype evolved which served to ascribe this kind of activity to Puerto Ricans, particularly to persons having few or no alternatives to factory operative jobs, and those facing additional disadvantages because of their youth and inexperience. Judging by the extent of service work among teenage and young adult women, it seems likely that the same kind of occupational ascription influenced their work involvement as well.

Compared with operative and service employment, fewer Puerto Rican men worked as laborers. Nevertheless, jobs typical of this category—freight, warehouse and stockroom handlers, constuction helpers, car washers, gardeners and groundskeepers—were as common as clerical or professional work among teenage and young adult men. The numbers of laborers at older ages surpassed the white-collar categories by a considerable margin, and increased at each point in time. The kinds of laborer work described have the common features of being very low-paid, often subject to slack periods, lay offs, part-time or piecework, with little or no promise of employment security or career advancement. As such, they offer no advantage over the factory and service jobs performed by most Puerto Ricans, and may be resorted to when the job market tightens and competition intensifies at the lowest levels of employment.

The "crafts" category or skilled manual work among Puerto Rican men gave the only clear sign of upward mobility in the data presented in Figure 15. These jobs were exemplified by mechanic and repair of refrigeration, heating and automobiles; dental laboratory technicians; metalsmiths, diesetters and molders; floor layers, carpet installers and tile setters. An employment career in crafts sometimes emerges from routine factory work as opportunities arise requiring special abilities for which experience as an operative may be useful. More typically, a worker's preparation involves vocational schooling and/or instruction while working as an apprentice in a specific line of activity. Manual dexterity and acceptance of unpleasant or messy conditions are rewarded by hourly wages generally higher than the pay received by operatives, and union membership is more common, which means a better potential for earning and job continuance.

Limited access to middle-class status through employment in crafts has become a more prominent aspect of Puerto Rican life than advancement to professional and administrative positions. This partly derives from tracking in the educational system, in which Puerto Ricans are generally steered toward vocational instruction and/or discouraged from following a college-preparatory curriculum. (29) But the underlying social factor is evidently structural; that is, Puerto Ricans are relegated to a position of low prestige and power in American society and the jobs they perform accord with this caste and colonized condition. Information to be presented shows that even among men aged 25-34 years (the only segment with a sizable number of professionals) the specific jobs performed are the lower-ranked within the occupational category. With such limited prospects for success, it seems reasonable that Puerto Rican youth envision work careers paying above-average wages for skilled manual work. These jobs have a limited scope for decision, creativity and recognition. But compared with work having greater power and prestige, access may be more readily arranged, and the material return for effort compensates for a lower social status.

INDUSTRIAL PATTERNS

Further analysis was completed regarding the production sectors or "industries" in which Puerto Ricans worked. In 1960, about a third of all employed Puerto Ricans were engaged in the manufacture of nondurable items (mainly textiles and apparel, plastics, paper and miscellaneous expendable products) and a quarter in the production of durables, such as fabricated metal objects, machinery and appliances. These proportions were fairly constant by gender and age, and consistent with the concentration of Puerto Ricans in the operative occupational category. Wholesale and retail trade accounted for about 15 percent of Puerto Rican workers, while personal services (private household, hotels, laundry, etc.) and professional services (medical, educational, legal and technical), each had about 7 percent. The general picture was one of heavy representation in factory production and only slight participation in the balance of sectors in economic production.

The comparative data in Figure 16 portray changes taking place since 1960, based on the differences between the percent distribution of Puerto Rican workers by industry at two time intervals, which indicate proportional declines or increases in each category. The most significant decline was in the nondurable manufacturing sector during the 1960s, particularly among workers younger than 25 years—a trend that continued in the 1970s, although less than before. Workers older than 25 years were less affected by the decline, probably because alternatives to factory work were more limited for them, than for persons entering the labor force and beginning work careers. A similar decline took place among workers in the manufacture of durables, but it was proportionately less than in the production of expendable items. Also, an increase occurred in the durable sector among workers aged 35 to 64, from 1970 to 1976. This finding was consistent with changes already mentioned in regard to occupational categories. As the number of operatives stabilized or declined, skilled manual jobs typical of durable production became more numerous.

From 1960 to 1976 the most notable expansion was in the professional service sector, particularly among workers younger than 25 years. There was a slight increase in public administration workers, as well. An even smaller percentage of Puerto Rican youth were shifting to work in the finance and business sectors. These changes are significant primarily because they represent a trend toward white-collar, bureaucratic forms of economic activity, and away from the predominance of manufacturing that characterized work performed by young Puerto Ricans in previous times. The shift from factory to office work in large-scale organizations was not extensive, however. At most, it involved one worker in five from one point in time to another.

In fact, changes among the production sectors were generally quite limited. Agriculture, mining, construction, transportation, communication and utilities employed relatively few Puerto Ricans and showed only negligible variations during the period considered. The extent of changes in the entire set of industrial categories can be summarized in the index of dissimilarity, which equals one-half the sum of percentage differences for two points in time, and represents the proportion of a group changing production sectors, creating change in the industrial distribution. Considering that 50 is the maximum score for change, the indexes of dissimilarity for the time and

16. INDUSTRY CHANGE RATES FOR PUERTO RICAN WORKERS BY AGE, 1960-70, 1970-76. DIFFERENCES IN PERCENT DISTRIBUTIONS: ■ 1960-1970 □ 1970-1976

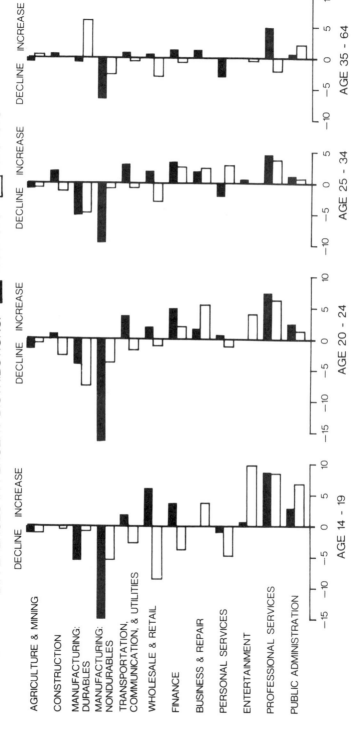

age groups presented in Figure 16 show only moderate to low levels of variation:

	14-19	20-24	25-34	35-64
1960-70	11.7	11.5	8.9	5.2
1970-76	13.9	9.2	5.6	4.0

These figures suggest that shifts among production sectors are important but do not broadly affect the Puerto Rican work force. The change rates also diminish with age, and show some decline from the 1960s to the 1970s. By implication, changes are now less frequent than in the past, and workers' engagement in production sectors approaches stability beyond 30 years of age. Therefore, the shift from factory to white-collar work is genuine, in that some younger Puerto Rican workers have moved in that direction and will likely remain in the finance, business, professional service and public administration sectors. But relative to the many others who began their work career as a laborer, attendant or factory worker and have stayed in this kind of job, white-collar work has been a limited alternative and is unlikely to become typical in the near future.

THREE SECTOR COMPARISON

"What kind of work will I do?" is often asked by young persons entering or returning to the labor force, and those thinking about changing their job. "Will I earn a decent living?" is a question that has a very important meaning. To provide some answers for Puerto Rican youth, we will now examine the kinds of jobs performed in relation to the production sectors just described. The production sectors will then be related to income received and measures of social status. For this purpose, data from the SIE were tabulated for workers younger than 35 years, in three major categories:

(a) manufacturing of durables and nondurables,
(b) wholesale, retail trade, finance, business and repair, and
(c) professional services and public administration.

Together, these categories encompass about 80 percent of the workers in 1976 and can be considered basic alternatives in work engagement. For brevity, they will be called "manufacturing, business and professional" industries.

The manufacturing sector was consistent with expectations, since most of the teenagers and young adults in this production line performed tasks already described as operative occupations. Close to half of each age category did the routine and repetitive factory work traditional for Puerto Ricans; that is, either assembly, "miscellaneous" machine operation, packing and wrapping of nondurables, or sewing and related tasks in textile and apparel production. The other half showed a certain progression by age from stock clerk and handler jobs to clerical work or semi-skilled operations and eventually to limited types of supervisory work. Among teenagers, occupations other than nondurable or textile operation mainly involved stock clerk and handler jobs. However, stock clerk and handler work diminished from a half to a quarter of the workers aged 20 to 24, and the remaining quarter either held such clerical jobs as bookkeeper or operative work in durable manufacturing. Stock clerk and handler jobs diminished further among workers aged 25 to 34. In this age group about 10 percent held jobs with some administrative responsibility, including sales representatives, personnel workers, supervisors of assembly work, and a few professionals occupied in manufacturing.

In the business sector only about 15 percent of Puerto Rican teenagers and young adults held sales clerk occupations. The remainder of each age group were about equally divided into three distinct occupational groups: clerical jobs (typist, secretary, file clerk and similar); food service jobs (dishwashers, kitchen helpers, counter attendants), and cleaning (mainly janitorial and car-washing). A small percentage of workers aged 20 to 24 held more prestigious jobs, such as bank teller and interviewer. Among those 25 to 34 years of age, 10 percent held either lower-level managerial positions (for example, buyers and sales representatives) or skilled manual jobs, such as carpet installer, jeweler, automobile mechanic, telephone installer and office machine operator.

The label "professional" proved misleading as a description of the types of work performed by Puerto Ricans in the professional and government service production sector. Only a small portion of teenage and young adult workers in this industrial category held jobs classfied as professional in the conventional listing of occupations: 8 percent, age 14-19; 25 percent, age 20-24 and 33 percent age 25-34. Most of the workers holding these professional jobs in the production of professional services were engaged in "helping" types of work: social workers, the clergy, recreational leaders, personnel and labor relations work—or they were elementary school teachers. The remainder of each age category in the professional industry sector resembled the remainder of the business sector, after sales clerk positions were considered. That is, the remainder was about equally divided into three distinct occupational groups: clerical jobs (for example: postal clerks, mail handlers and teacher's aides); cleaning jobs, and lower-level health service jobs, such as nursing aides, orderlies, hospital attendants, and trainees, child and elderly care assistants. Television and movie portrayals of Puerto Rican youth as helpers of institutionalized persons therefore seem indicative of statistical facts, and the evolution of bilingual education programs in the mid-1970s is visible in the frequency of teacher's aide positions. (30) Generally speaking, young adults in professional and government service production were engaged in low prestige level, person-to-person assistance types of work, or in community-related jobs.

INCOME PATTERNS

"How much does this job pay?" is a crucial question asked by young people considering a work career. Data from the SIE tabulations on the earnings of Puerto Rican youth were summarized in Table 17, according to the three major production sectors just discussed. In general, teenagers earned very little, as many worked only on a seasonal or part-time basis. Income received by workers aged 20 to 24 averaged less than $5200 yearly or $100 weekly and $2.50 hourly—assuming full-time, full-year employment as a criterion of work involvement. Information to be presented in the following chapter will show that many of these workers held only part-time jobs or stretches of full-time work for less than 52 weeks yearly. This may account for the low income levels, although working for less than the minimum wage level (nationally about $2.30 an hour in 1976) has been common among Puerto Rican workers who are paid in cash. (31) Median annual income figures for workers aged 25 to 34 were higher than for younger persons, but their earnings were about average for Puerto Rican workers of all ages. This suggests important limitations on earning abilities as people approach the life-cycle peak of worker productivity in their thirties.

A comparison of mean annual earnings by production sector reveals that factory work in manufacturing paid more than business and professional service production to workers younger than 25 years. But this advantage was reversed among workers 25 to 34 years of age. The nature and responsibilities of factory work seldom change during the employment career of the average worker, and chances for promotion and significant pay raises are very limited. Most factory workers are therefore locked into a certain income level from the beginning of employment in their early twenties. In contrast, workers in business and professional service production begin their employment careers at typically low wage levels and subsequently earn more as experience is gained and promotions take place. (32)

Although Puerto Rican white-collar workers eventually earn more than factory workers, their income levels were not high, relative to income standards in the United States. In 1975 the median income earned by all white-collar workers was $14,920 for men and $8,288 for women, and the median earned by all workers aged 25-34 in all occupations was $13,240 for men and $8,939 for women. The figures in Table 17 show that even in the most favorable circumstances Puerto Rican women and men (considered together) earned less than these amounts. Moreover, Puerto Rican workers earning more than the median for their age and sector category were mainly clustered just above the average. At best, a quarter of Puerto Rican workers 25 to 34 years of age in the professional service sector earned $10,000 or more, which compares with 45 percent for all male workers in the United States and 13 percent for all women, regardless of industry sector. (33)

"If the pay isn't much higher, why even think about an alternative to factory work?" Again, a typical question posed by youth finds some answer in generalizations traditional to the social sciences. Although individual motivation in work careers varies widely in nature and intensity, aggregate patterns show that certain rewards other than money are perceived as available in business and professional services, principally the prestige factors of power and social status. White-collar work is socially valued more than manual occupations--a difference having implications for most aspects of a person's lifestyle, including marriage, living arrangements, apparel and recreation.

As noted in Table 17 the occupations recorded in the SIE were coded for social value by the U.S. Commission on Civil Rights, enabling researchers to analyze the nonmonetary significance of jobs. The same procedure was followed in regard to the 1960 and 1970 Censuses, providing a historical background for considering the prestige attributed to the work performed by minorities and

17. ANNUAL INCOME AND OCCUPATIONAL PRESTIGE INDICATORS FOR PUERTO RICAN WORKERS, BY SELECTED AGE GROUPS AND INDUSTRY SECTORS, 1975-76.

INDICATORS	14-19	20-24	25-34	INDUSTRY SECTOR*
MEDIAN	$936	$4651	$5203	Manufacturing
INCOME	$898	$3089	$7025	Business
	$612	$3439	$8185	Professional
PERCENT				
EARNING	0.0	17.3	18.3	Manufacturing
$10,000 OR	0.0	7.9	17.6	Business
MORE	0.0	8.6	24.3	Professional
MEAN JOB	29	29	29	Manufacturing
PRESTIGE	27	31	31	Business
SCORE**	34	35	46	Professional
PERCENT WITH				
PRESTIGE	0.0	1.8	7.6	Manufacturing
SCORES	0.0	0.0	12.8	Business
OF 50 OR MORE	7.9	26.1	35.3	Professional

* Manufacturing refers to the production of durable and nondurable goods. Business includes Census industry listings of wholesale and retail trade, finance, insurance, and real estate, business and repair services. Public administration was joined with professional services to form the third category.

** Prestige scores were coded for each occupation and ranged from a high of 88 for physicians to a low of 1.5 for bootblacks. Documentation and comparative data for Puerto Ricans and other workers are provided by U.S. Commission on Civil Rights, Social Indicators of Equality for Minorities and Women, Washington, D.C., 1978:34-38.

women in the United States. In terms of a range of values from 1.5 to 88, the mean prestige scores for Puerto Rican workers of all ages were:

	1960	1970	1976
Male	28.8	31.2	32.1
Female	31.0	33.9	32.9

These figures show little or no advance during the sixteen year period considered in the Commission's publication.

The question posed here is whether young adult Puerto Rican workers (especially those holding jobs in business and professional industries) differed from the stationary condition just described for all Puerto Rican workers. It can be generally said in answer that the averages did not differ notably, except among workers 25 to 34 years of age, in professional and government services. The mean prestige scores for all other age and industry categories approximated the figures published by the Civil Rights Commission for all Puerto Rican workers. Minor features in this comparison include the fact that prestige scores for workers in manufacturing did not change at all from teenagers to older persons. Prestige scores for workers in the business sector also leveled off beyond age 20, and at a slightly higher figure than for workers in manufacturing.

The figures on percent of workers having prestige scores of at least 50 show that a small number of Puerto Ricans in manufacturing and business eventually advanced in social standing to a middle-class level, exemplified by the following prestige scores: accountant (61), credit worker (56), secretary (48), dietician (47), and electrician (44). Consistent with the information on household income presented at the beginning of Chapter 2 and the results analyzed up to this point, most Puerto Rican workers begin their work career well below this level and stay in low-paid jobs with little change or advancement. The exception is not necessarily ruled out; that is, a few workers manage to reach moderately prestigious positions in factories, stores and offices. Together with a somewhat larger proportion of those working in schools, hospitals and other public institutions, the successful make up an elite considered middle-class in the social stratification of the United States.

DISCUSSION

The data presented were organized to facilitate a retrospective view of the type of work performed by Puerto Rican youth since the large-scale migration to the continent in the 1950s. In most labor force studies, an analysis of occupation and industry follows a detailed look at basic employment patterns, the topic of the next Chapter. Here, the order was reversed because discrimination remains a common feature of the Puerto Rican labor experience in the United States. Most Puerto Rican workers are assigned by social and economic forces beyond their control to certain types of jobs—either traditional factory work or low-level service and clerical positions near the bottom of the pay and prestige scales of employment. This knowledge helps one to understand the dismal picture emerging from such measures as unemployment rates, and why the household income data already discussed were so depressed.

Now and then an individual Puerto Rican may avoid the discrimination trap, gain a steady, prestigious job, and earn a "decent" living. From a collective viewpoint, however, this is clearly a statistical rarity. Generally speaking, Puerto Ricans perform the least desired jobs in each of the major production sectors in which they are represented: manufacturing, business, and professional services. This remains true even in those segments of the population that would be expected to change significantly, according to the assimilation perspective. For example, low-paid, low-prestige, low-responsibility and dead-end jobs remained typical even among young Puerto Ricans born in the United States, persons who had always lived where they were in 1976; those speaking English as a usual language, and high school graduates.

Strictly speaking, the occupation and industrial data do not provide a direct measure of labor market conditions. Theoretically, the jobs people hold also reflect their employment preferences, their skills and such factors as chance in finding and maintaining employment. But this does not invalidate the information on jobs as a indicator of labor market conditions; it only reduces the strength of the influence that can be attributed to the availability or lack of opportunity in certain types of work, and other "structural" aspects of employment. To deny any connection between the jobs people hold and the social circumstances in which they seek and find employment would imply much greater error than the mistake of placing too much importance on labor market conditions.

The most controversial element of the linkage between occupational data and labor market conditions are assertions and inferences regarding discrimination. Information from such public sources as the Census and the SIE does not provide a direct measure of differences in disposition among employers to hire and promote Puerto Ricans (as compared with other workers), nor the existence of informal barriers to employment deriving from negative mental images or stereotypes of a Puerto Rican worker. Experience tells us that inequality based on racial or ethnic identity is nevertheless as operative in job placement and advancement as a candidate's qualifications and willingness to work. Whatever fragments of factual information are available on discrimination confirm this general impression. For example, a Roper survey in 1982 found Puerto Ricans to be the second least desirable group in the United States in a field of fifteen groups presented to respondents. Only 17 percent of the persons interviewed agreed that Puerto Ricans were good for the United States, 43 percent said Puerto Ricans were bad for the nation, and 40 percent had mixed feelings or did not know. (34) Therefore, it seems reasonable to suppose that if Puerto Ricans are not represented in a certain job category, their absence signfies that among other factors, discrimination explains the lack of employment.

For example: why were so few Puerto Rican youth employed as sales clerks in the business production sector? For millions of teenagers and young adults in the United States, a job as a sales clerk provides an important way of entering the labor force and gaining work experience of value in a sales career, or in preparation for a variety of jobs that require knowledge and skills in handling merchandise, customers and money. In this instance, it cannot be argued that Puerto Ricans live far away from major retail sales areas, because they are located in major consumer markets--New York City, Philadelphia and Chicago.

The consistent hiring pattern among retail firms involves the selection of sales clerks from applicants who personally approach the manager or personnel department representative, seeking work. This enables the decision-makers or their delegates to evaluate an applicant's appearance and language, in accord with the image they would like to project toward customers. Typically, the walk-in applicant is asked to complete a questionnaire sufficiently detailed as to provide a justification for disqualifying almost everyone on some basis other than race, ethnicity, gender, age or personality. Simply stated, employers hire the applicants whom they like or feel would be attractive to customers, easy to get along with, and trustworthy.

An elaborate and costly social science research project could be organized to test the hypotheses that:

(a) intake clerks in personnel departments of large retail firms generally screen out applicants with Spanish surnames or accents in speech, those listing Puerto Rico as their birthplace, graduates of certain high schools, and individuals who "look Puerto Rican."

(b) small shops hire persons resembling the owners or managers, who are almost always white and "mainstream" American.

(c) compared with other applicants who do not fully accord with the desired image, Puerto Ricans tend to be among the least favorable type of applicant in the decision-maker's mind.

The data collected would then be analyzed and related to the scant representation of Puerto Ricans among sales clerk workers. Most likely, this would "prove" the existence and effectiveness of discrimination.

The time, energy and money invested in the research would add scientific rigor to conclusions that can be validly made by simply observing the application and rejection process. Among persons repeatedly observing it, the following sociological generalization can be reliably made: "Puerto Ricans are not wanted as sales clerks." The best information source for the observations are the applicants, themselves. After a long and arduous effort of applying at various stores, not hearing from them leaves one with the impression that the jobs are not open to you as a Puerto Rican. Looking around the store to see who was hired serves to validate one's impression. The sales clerks are not Puerto Rican.

Once the impression is validated and the conclusion reached, the logical follow-up idea becomes: "why even bother applying for a sales clerk position?" As a practical application, the experienced job seeker looks for a more promising type of job, the kind of employment perceived to be open to Puerto Ricans. For example: kitchen helper, hospital attendant and the other jobs which the SIE statistics showed to be the principal ways of earning a living among Puerto Rican youth. The discrimination process has thus moved full circle to the applicants themselves in their approach to the job market. Because very few Puerto Ricans bother applying for sales clerk positions, almost none of them will be hired. In the meantime, the alternative types of jobs are increasingly identified as "Puerto Rican" by the general public.

Breaking out of job stereotypes is a policy more easily proposed by labor economists concerned with discrimination, than a practical solution for Puerto Rican youth facing unemployment. In any case, the teenagers and young adults who apply for jobs different from those considered "Puerto Rican" have little or no power to influence the judgment of potential employers, let alone change the negative image evoked by an applicant identified as Puerto Rican. As in the case of a Puerto Rican child who is alienated, bored and uninvolved in an indifferent, if not hostile school environment, blaming the victim offers a convenient evasion from consideration of structural changes that would make a difference in the outcome of the discrimination process.

Until recently, the principal way of changing structural conditions limiting employment chances for Puerto Rican youth was thought to be affirmative action, or a deliberate effort to recruit and hire minorities, sometimes following specific goals and timetables. Our data make it plain that affirmative action was not effective in opening opportunities for this particular group. To some extent, the failure can be attributed to strategies used by employers for reducing government pressure to apply affirmative action guidelines. For example, many retail firms have decentralized their hiring procedures into units smaller than the cutoff affected by law. Advertisements including "equal opportunity employer" and related phrases appear in newspapers, but entry-level positions are described vaguely enough to not refer specifically to the jobs actually available. (35) Continued reliance on the screening of walk-in applicants has enabled employers to select the persons whom they like and feel should have the jobs.

Certain additional factors have further reduced the efficacy of affirmative action for Puerto Ricans. In the racial and ethnic queue of competition among minority applicants for scarce positions, Puerto Ricans are not often preferred. (36) Comprehensive and vaguely defined categories such as "Spanish-speaking," and "Hispanic" have provided employers with a flexibility to hire individuals who are not genuinely indigenous minorities, or to not hire Puerto Ricans. The "Spanish-surname" criterion excludes about 35 percent of Puerto Ricans, who have surnames other than Spanish in origin. (37) Variations among Puerto Ricans that directly affect employment chances have remained untouched by affirmative action policies. Included here are skin color, physical appearance and clothing styles, gender, age and degree of "Americanization." The statement, "We hired a Puerto Rican, but not like all the rest" epitomizes the reasons why all the rest remained disadvantaged by affirmative action.

Affirmative action could be more effective for Puerto Ricans, if certain changes were made:

1. Deliberate recruitment and hiring efforts should be specific to Puerto Ricans, including both continental and island populations as a human resource potential. At first glance, this seems to place U.S. Puerto Ricans at a disadvantage; but migration from Puerto Rico involves a continual flow of job seekers,

anyway; and the circular U.S./Puerto Rico movement has gradually created a floating labor force, distinct from long- term residents of continent and island, which represents a major employment need in both places.

2. Specific goals should be keyed to the metropolitan areas in which Puerto Ricans are represented in significant numbers and are a constituency for policy makers. For this purpose, diagnostic research is needed, not just to "prove" discrimination by reason of the absence of Puerto Rican workers, but more importantly, to identify the kinds of jobs that could be filled by Puerto Ricans, given the human resource characterisitcs of the population.

3. The institutional emphasis should be on specific employers having a sufficiently large-scale line organization to offer promotion possibilities for Puerto Rican youth hired for entry-level employment. Their identity and selection for attention in affirmative action should be made known to Puerto Ricans and news of progress disseminated. A community-based effort in both continent and island, to boycott the products of the companies that fail to meet the specific goals would help to call public attention to the employment difficulties experienced by Puerto Ricans.

4. Strategies that have proved effective in the placement and advancement of Puerto Ricans must be strengthened. The most important is the kinship, barrio and place-of-origin networks developed by Puerto Ricans themselves to fill needs left unattended by certain employment agencies, job counseling services, training programs and similar activities. Money and energy should be devoted to facilitate raising the consciousness of Puerto Rican workers to issues of collective job experience, especially the problems faced by youth, persons age 45 and older, and women with household responsibilities.

5. An agency controlled by Puerto Ricans should assume responsibility for monitoring the effectiveness of public efforts to improve employment opportunities, including job counseling and training programs. The same agency should receive complaints of discriminatory treatment. Although negotiation with employers and litigation may be possible only in a very limited number of cases, the accumulated documentation would provide valuable material for public disclosure of inequities in hiring and promotion.

6. To the extent that they operate effectively, the job-placement functions of community organizations should be strengthened. Otherwise, efforts should be redirected to the activities just mentioned, and, generally speaking, to the orientation of Puerto Rican workers for the labor market in the particular vicinity served by the organization.

These suggestions assume that neither that United States government nor the American public can be counted on to have a strong enough interest in Puerto Rican employment problems, to make a difference in the 1980s. Whatever help is forthcoming from outside the community should, of course, be utilized. But the policy approach taken on the basis of over a decade of decline and disappointment reduces basically to collective self-reliance. To the extent that we increase our awareness of discrimination and become actively involved in seeking solutions to employment problems, the future will look hopeful.

4. EMPLOYMENT FACTORS

Being limited to certain kinds of occupations and to a work situation of low prestige and earnings are only part of the consequences of assignment by the American economy to "Puerto Rican" jobs. Jobs considered Puerto Rican have the common feature of employment insecurity; that is, no assurance of continuation from time to time, nor schedule fixed to full-time, full-year engagement. The details of seasonal and part-time work among Puerto Rican youth will be discussed after looking at the more fundamental topic of employment—whether a person has a job or not. Since most opportunities for jobs other than Puerto Rican are closed for one or another reason, the squeeze on Puerto Rican jobs makes them scarce as well. The competition is especially great when the nation's unemployment rate is high and Puerto Rican jobs also attract non-Puerto Ricans, or when a sudden influx of new workers occurs, as when refugees or other disadvantaged people arrive in cities where Puerto Ricans live.

At the time of the SIE in 1976 and in 1982 when this book was finished, a jobless condition approaching 10 percent of the US labor force meant that some 10 million non-Puerto Ricans were looking for work. Many unemployed persons would gladly accept a job having less prestige, income and stability than would be expected in times of prosperity. The time between 1976 and 1982 was hardly a boom period of employment for persons seeking jobs below a middle-class level of work. For example, entry-level sales or office clerk jobs and manual employment have been sought by white college graduates. (38) Social and economic depression has intensified retrenchment and heightened competition for jobs, with the result that many persons who need, desire and seek work have experienced long-term stretches of unemployment. Those hardest hit by the employment squeeze are persons entering or returning to the labor force and workers with disadvantages in the labor market. The jobless situation of so many Puerto Rican youth is therefore an extreme example of the general lack of employment prospects for youth, minorities and women in the United States.

LABOR FORCE PARTICIPATION

Almost all of our knowledge about people's economic characteristics and work orientation is based on information gathered according to the nation's concept of "labor force." By government definition, labor force participation refers to persons currently having or actively seeking nondomestic work for monetary renumeration. The SIE labor force questions began with the question: "what was . . . doing most of last week?" A respondent was considered a labor force participant if one of the first three alternatives applied: "working / with a job but not at work / looking for work / keeping house / going to school/unable to work / retired/other (specify)." For respondents not reporting "working," there were follow-up questions intended to reduce classification errors: "Did . . . do any work at all last week, not counting work around the house?" "Did . . .have a job or business from which he (sic) was temporarily absent or on lay off last week?" "Has . . . been looking for work during the past 4 weeks?" The bottom line for inclusion in the labor force was a "yes"answer to the last question—which required one to specify the method used to find work (public employment agency, etc.). In effect, the labor force definition reduced to persons either working or having some type of job commitment during the week previous to the Survey, or reporting a specific kind of effort to find paid nondomestic employment. (39)

Despite some variations in questionnaire wording and specifications, the labor force definition has remained essentially the same during the past quarter century. Throughout that time, labor force participation has been nearly universal among adult men from their early twenties until retirement about age 65, except for full-time students and the physically or mentally disabled. Since housework and family care remain excluded from the standard labor force definition, women's participation in official statistics on work has been comparatively limited. During the 1970s, however, a departure from tradition meant a slightly reduced labor force involvement among men (attributable mainly to extended schooling and early retirement) and notable increases in women's work outside the home.

The labor force participation of Puerto Ricans in the United States has differed from the general pattern in several basic ways. Table

18 shows that since 1960 the participation rates of both men and women have been lower than average for the nation. Among Puerto Rican men, a decline in labor force engagement has taken place—parallel to the general decline among men—but with a consistent 4 to 5 percent gap. In 1960 Puerto Rican women had a labor force participation rate close to the average for all women in the United States; but this measure declined significantly during the 1960s and has stabilized since then at a level of only one third of adult women.

18. PUERTO RICANS AND THE TOTAL UNITED STATES POPULATION: CIVILIAN LABOR FORCE PARTICIPATION RATES BY GENDER, FOR SELECTED YEARS, 1960-78

| | POPULATION 16 YEARS AND OLDER (*) | | | | | |
| | men | | | women | | |
	US total	Puerto Rican	differ- ential	US total	Puerto Rican	differ- ential
1960	84.0	(79.6)*	−4.4	37.8	(36.3)*	−1.5
1970	80.6	75.2	−5.4	43.4	32.3	−11.2
1974	79.4	75.7	−3.7	45.7	33.7	12.0
1975	78.5	73.5	−5.0	46.4	33.5	−12.9
1976	78.1	73.1	−5.0	47.4	34.9	−12.5
1977	77.2	71.9	−5.3	47.7	(29.9)*	−17.8
1978	78.5	72.6	−5.9	49.4	32.4	−17.0

Sources: Census and Current Population Reports previously noted except 1976: SIE tabulations; 1978: U.S. Bureau of the Census, Statistical Abstract: 387-9.
*1960 figures are for population 14 years and older; in view of its inconsistency with the times series, the 1977 rate for Puerto Rican women may be in error.

Since the national trend was toward increased women's involvement in nondomestic work, the gap between Puerto Rican and total labor force participation rates became larger. By the late 1970s the gap had reached a 17 percentage-point difference, and stood in sharp contrast with the increased labor force participation rates of other Hispanic women. (40)

In every population the need, desire and opportunity to work varies with life cycle stages from youth to old age. A determination of reasons for the gap in labor force participation must therefore begin with data refinements by age groups. Table 19 serves this purpose by presenting participation rates for Puerto Rican men and

19. LABOR FORCE PARTICIPATION RATES OF PUERTO RICANS AND DIFFERENTIALS FROM THE TOTAL UNITED STATES POPULATION, BY AGE AND GENDER: 1960, 1970, 1976.

| | PUERTO RICANS | | | | | |
| | MEN | | | WOMEN | | |
AGE	1960	1970	1976	1960	1970	1976
16-19	(34.4)*	42.2	30.9	(24.3)*	27.4	35.6
20-24	89.5	79.0	92.4	45.0	39.5	48.9
25-34	91.6	88.6	87.6	39.1	29.9	37.3
35-44	91.6	80.0	84.2	43.9	37.4	35.6
45-64	81.8	78.2	64.1	33.4	33.4	27.1
65 +	23.0	22.6	9.9	4.9	8.5	0.0

DIFFERENTIALS FROM RATES OF
UNITED STATES TOTAL POPULATION

| | MEN | | | WOMEN | | |
AGE	1960	1970	1976	1960	1970	1976
16-19	(− 21.2)*	− 15.3	− 29.4	(− 14.8)*	− 16.3	− 14.2
20-24	+ 0.6	− 6.1	+ 7.2	− 1.1	− 18.0	− 16.1
25-34	− 4.8	− 6.4	− 6.6	+ 3.3	− 14.9	− 19.6
35-44	− 4.8	− 15.7	− 10.4	+ 0.8	− 13.5	− 22.0
45-64	− 8.6	− 12.1	− 18.8	− 10.5	− 15.5	− 20.9
65 +	− 9.2	− 3.2	− 9.5	− 5.5	− 0.7	− 7.8

Sources: Census, Current Population Reports and SIE Tabulations.
*1960 figures are for persons aged 14-19.

women in major age categories and a comparison with the United States total, from 1960 to 1976.

During the period considered, the most drastic declines in participation rates occurred among middle-aged and older Puerto Ricans. From a level of 82 percent work involvement in 1960, men aged 45 to 64 lost 18 percentage points—reaching 64 percent in 1976, which meant that almost one-third were neither working nor actively looking for a job by SIE definition. Women aged 35 and older had a proportionately equivalent decline in labor force participation. Although a loss of 7 or 8 percentage points may look smaller in comparison with the percentage decline among men, in relation to women's lower participation levels the negative significance was proportionately the same or even greater. For both men and women, the differentials from the participation rates of the entire U.S. population generally grew larger from 1960 to 1976. This shows that the labor force gap was widening and that the work experience of Puerto Ricans 35 years and older was markedly divergent from the national pattern.

Several life cycle factors strongly motivate the average middle-aged person to work on a full-time, full-year basis. The typical alternatives to work which may appeal to certain younger persons—education, leisure activities, marriage and family formation—have much less influence on the mature man or woman. The reasons for working become quite compelling, instead. In the commentary on Table 17 we noted that the income received by Puerto Ricans "levels off" by age 30, with the possible exception of workers in professional industries. With sharply rising costs of living and the eroding effects of inflation in the 1970s, a steady income level signified a progressively weaker economic situation. The poverty and financial depression described in Chapter 2 further indicates an overwhelming need among Puerto Ricans for some way of earning a living and more money than received at present.

For the mature person, the need for work is strengthened as responsibilities and uncertainties become greater. Generally speaking, both men and women face high dependency costs from raising children, caring for their parents, and providing for themselves. In addition, many Puerto Rican workers over 30 years of age do not have health insurance for themselves and their family, as a fringe benefit of employment. Serious illnesses and disabilities usually imply a severe and continuing crisis that can be remedied only by more work and more income. As employment opportunities diminish with age, many people approaching retirement must solve the fundamental problem of economic survival. The labor force participation rates for persons age 65 and older (Table 19) show a marked decline from 1960 to 1976, proportionately greater than among the middle-aged. The older generation of Puerto Rican migrants is basically composed of people who originated their work careers as farm laborers or housewives and more recently have been employed (if at all) in a series of manual jobs with a high turnover factor and little or nothing in terms of unemployment or disability compensation or pensions. Many were not eligible for participation in the social security program and remain so by reason of unemployment or the nature of their jobs. As a general result, middle- and older-aged Puerto Ricans must often turn to their children and young relatives for support.

Our statistics do not offer any direct information on the effect of this pressure on Puerto Rican youth, nor about the continuance of the traditional expectations of family responsibility and care for people advanced in age. However, men 20-24 and women 20-34 showed increased labor force participation in 1976, compared with 1970. This represented a recovery from a decline in the 1960s, a return to previous levels of work commitment, and an exception to the general participation decline. Puerto Rican men 20-24 exceeded the national average for their group by 7 percentage points, resulting partly from less involvement in postsecondary education than among other young men and a stronger work commitment. From Chapter 1 we recall that during the 1970s many of the young women represented here migrated from Puerto Rico and/or assumed sole responsibility for households. Although some increased labor force participation was evident among young women, the extent of self-reliance and responsibility implied by the household data should have meant an even greater level of work involvement. Compared with the total U.S. female population aged 20-39, a 16-20 percentage gap seems to say that many Puerto Rican young women found considerable difficulties in "actively seeking work;" that is, in relating to the job market and entering the labor force.

TRANSITION TO ADULTHOOD

A more detailed examination of labor force entry and initial participation was completed for 1976, based on a tabulation of employment charactertistics by three-year age groups, the smallest interval possible for this purpose, using SIE data. For teenagers and young adults, looking for work is often viewed in relation to attending school—as a supportive activity (the typical "summer" job) or an alternative to school, the next step after graduation, or some combination of these. However, finding a job and being at work were not easy for minority youth in the 1970s and early 1980s, especially if they lacked the social advantages which facilitate searching and being hired, such factors as having parents with advanced education or contacts with potential employers. (41) The data illustrated in Figure 20 relate school attendance and work engagement to being in the labor force, which includes looking for work and having a job but not actually working, in addition to work, itself.

20. PUERTO RICAN MEN AND WOMEN AGE 14-31:
PERCENT ATTENDING SCHOOL, IN THE LABOR FORCE AND AT WORK, 1976.

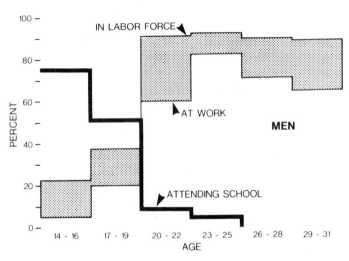

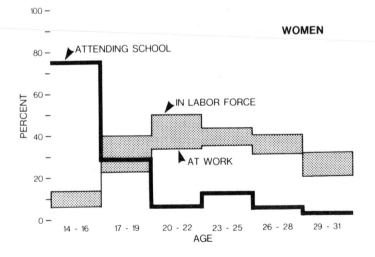

A quarter of the Puerto Rican teenagers had left school by ages 14 to 16, at least two years younger than 18, or the average age of secondary school graduation in the total United States population. Since one third of Puerto Rican students are delayed at least one grade in their schooling, most 17 to 19 years of age would be attending school, if graduation were universal. But at that age level about half of the men and more than seventy percent of the women had left school—a substantial proportion resembling the "push-out" or "drop-out" rates found in previous research. (42) Although fewer young women continued attending school than young men 20 to 22 years of age, they returned to school in larger numbers in their mid-to late twenties. Although the eventual result may be about the same level of schooling for men and women, the attainment process for women is less in step with the sequence of graduation and initial work experience, which is socially expected in the case of men and sets a standard for career development.

Labor force participation began before age 17 for one in five Puerto Rican teenagers. It then increased sharply to about 40 percent at ages 17 to 19, with a slightly higher percentage of women economically active, than men. At ages 20 to 22, women's work commitment reached a peak of about 50 percent, compared with over 90 percent for men of the same age. In the mid-to-late twenties, labor force participation consistently declined among women, but remained in the vicinity of 90 percent among men. These differences reflect social expectations regarding gender roles in marriage and family formation. They also show that a substantial proportion of Puerto Rican young women do not have labor force experience, which would be of potential value later in their life cycle. Considering that at least half of the women will eventually have sole responsibility for their households, the lack of economic activity during younger years will likely be a disadvantage when they enter the labor force.

The percentage of Puerto Rican teenagers (men and women) in the labor force was lower than the proportion not attending school. This shows that certain persons who had left school were neither working nor looking for work—which raises many questions about the social nature of the transition to adulthood. For example, how much voluntary idleness and time out for adventure can we suppose in a population notably affected by poverty? To what extent were Puerto Rican youth involved in activities for which the SIE questionnaire had no categories; such things as helping their parents, adjusting to the effects of migration, learning about their environment, working in quasi-legal ways or serving time in institutions of adjudication and correction? Whatever the answers may be, an important fact derived from the SIE was that almost half of the Puerto Rican teenagers and young adults not in the labor force claimed they wanted a regular job. This apparent contradiction may be explained by the discouragement said to influence older persons from continuing to seek work during long periods of unemployment. The discouraged worker envisions little or no chance of being hired and is thus inclined to accept a jobless condition as not having a likely solution in the near future.(43)

The large differences between the percentages of Puerto Ricans in the labor force and those actually working certainly imply a discouraging outlook for employment. Persons age 20 to 22 represent a transitional stage following the large-scale exit from school and preceding establishment in a work career. Over 90 percent of the men in that age category were in the labor force, but only 60 percent were actually working. Also, labor force participation reached its highest level among women—half of those 20 to 22 of age—but only one third were employed. The many who were seeking but not finding work were likely experiencing frustration in their efforts and eventually scaling down their aspirations to low-paid and menial occupations, and part-time or seasonal employment. Some were probably forming a career orientation that assumed uncertainty and lack of job opportunities as their usual expectation. To the extent that such experiences were anticipated by younger Puerto Ricans, discouragement spread and tended to provide an influence in the negative process of abandoning efforts to look for full-time, yearly employment.

Compared with all other age groups, Puerto Ricans 23 to 25 years of age had the least unemployment. However, by ages 29 to 31 the decline in labor force participation and the gap between labor force participation and the full potential for economic activity began to appear, for both men and women. The transition from youth to adulthood was thus marked by a problematic period of entry in which leaving school before graduation and not finding steady work was the common experience of most Puerto Ricans. We know that the eventual placement meant low-paid, low-prestige and uncertain employment, which seems to set in motion a life pattern of diminished motivation for seeking work and reduced chances for progressive advancement in a work career.

UNEMPLOYMENT

The official United States definition of unemployment is limited to persons who report "actively seeking work" during the four weeks prior to a Current Population Survey or the decennial Census. This does not include discouraged potential workers, nor those classified as "with a job but not at work," for being laid off or taking time to look for another job. The unemployment rate (the percentage of the labor force reported as unemployed by this definition) is one of the most frequently cited statistics produced by the government. It is generally considered to measure problems in economic well-being and the economy's capacity to absorb the demand for employment. Above a minimum level said to be inevitable because of job changes and labor force entry and return, the unemployment rate signals economic hardship involving serious difficulties for people in finding and keeping jobs. (44)

Because of the cyclical nature of the unemployment rate, intergroup comparisons should be made in a uniform time series of observations. However, unemployment rates have not been routinely available for Puerto Ricans until recent years and even now the validity and precision of the data remain in question. (45) We are therefore restricted to comparisons of data from the 1960 and 1970 Censuses and the SIE, as summarized in Table 21. In general, these figures show high rates of unemployment, particularly in 1976, shortly after the total U.S. population had reached its highest unemployment rate since the economic depression of the 1930s and nearly eight million people were seeking work—more than twice the annual jobless totals typical of the 1941 to 1969 period. (46) In comparison with 1976, 1960 and 1970 were years of low to moderate unemployment in the United States economy, and thus serve to describe the jobless situation of Puerto Ricans under somewhat more favorable market conditions.

As in the total United States population, unemployment varied by age among Puerto Ricans. Teenagers and young adults 20 to 24 years of age had very high unemployment rates, which reflect lack of work experience, barriers to job placement and career development, the temporal nature and uncertainty of jobs typically performed by youth, and many factors already mentioned. In 1976, almost half of the Puerto Rican teenagers in the labor force were jobless, about three times the unemployment rate of 15 percent for majority male teenagers. Except for black females, the Puerto

Rican teenage unemployment rates were higher than those for other minority groups, which varied from 24 to 48 percent. (47) As shown in Table 21, compared with the total of all these population segments, the Puerto Rican teenage unemployment rate was more than double, clearly indicating a severely depressed and disadvantaged situation.

21. UNEMPLOYMENT INDICATORS FOR PUERTO RICANS BY AGE AND GENDER, 1960, 1970, 1976.

	UNEMPLOYED PUERTO RICANS					
	1960		1970		1976	
A. Rate (Percent of Labor Force) by Age:	men	women	men	women	men	women
14-19*	19.3	15.8	15.7	15.6	48.5	39.3
20-24	10.2	12.3	7.0	7.9	19.7	26.8
25-34	8.2	10.3	4.8	8.6	14.2	15.1
14-64*	9.4	10.6	5.6	8.6	13.5	21.3
B. Ratio, Puerto Rican to Total U.S. Population						
14-19*	1.8	1.6	1.4	1.3	2.7	2.3
20-24	1.3	1.8	1.1	1.2	1.6	2.2
25-34	1.9	1.8	1.6	1.6	2.1	2.1
14-64*	1.9	2.0	1.4	1.6	1.7	2.4

*Data are for ages 16-19 and 16-64 in 1976; rates for ages 14-64 are standardized by age of U.S. total population. Sources as previously noted, and U.S. Census Bureau. 1960 Census Detailed Characteristics, PC(1)- 1D:487; 1970 Census, Subject Reports, PC(2)-6A Employment Status and Work Experience: 1-2; Statistical Abstract, 1977:354-360.

Although the Puerto Rican unemployment rates diminished in the age categories from 20 to 34, they remained about twice the rates for the U.S. total population. Moreover, compared with 1960 and 1970, the gap between Puerto Rican youth unemployment and that of the same age segments of the nation's population had become greater. A worsening of employment was especially apparent from 1970 to 1976, when the ratios of Puerto Rican to total U.S. population practically doubled for teenagers and persons age 20 to 24. The negative impact on the Puerto Rican community can be assessed in terms of this population's age composition, already described. Compared proportionately with the U.S. total population and most of its major segments, relatively more Puerto Ricans began their labor force experience in the 1970s. The generation of children born to the migrants of the 1950s and the continued flow of youth from Puerto Rico combined to make the 14 to 24 age groups exceptionally numerous and significant among continental Puerto Ricans.

Another large segment of the Puerto Rican population will reach the entry stage of labor force participation in the remaining years of this century. Since unemployment rates have not significantly declined since 1976, the outlook is very deplorable, by almost any criterion. Should the conditions analyzed here continue, the continental Puerto Rican population will be eventually include many people having a chronic inability to support themselves and their dependents in a standard of living considered minimal in the United States. At best, it will be a populace with a sense of deprivation stemming from years of frustration, disappointment and despair.

Perhaps the most telling statistics in Table 21 are the ratios of Puerto Rican to total U.S. unemployment for ages 14 to 64. These figures are based on unemployment rates that were standardized by the age composition of the total U.S. population. That is, they were made to show levels of unemployment as though Puerto Ricans had the same age composition as the U.S. total population. The adjustment shows that regardless of age, Puerto Rican unemployment is significantly higher than the nation's rate, at all of the dates considered. The figures signify that youth employment problems are not resolved with advancement in the life cycle and work careers. Being Puerto Rican implies a lifelong disadvantage in the job market, and there is no evidence of improvement. The only changes were a slight decline from 1960 to 1970, followed by an increase from 1970 to 1976, which runs parallel to the pattern for teenagers and young adults. Although more recent data are unavailable in sufficient detail for updated comparisons, the general economic adversity of the 1980s will likely mean a continued or even worsened employment situation for Puerto Ricans of all ages.

UNDEREMPLOYMENT

Merely having a job does not assure a worker of achieving personal aspirations or even of having a greater return than needed for survival. The depressed income of Puerto Ricans is partly explained by the continuing underemployment experienced by a significant portion of workers. The term "underemployment" has been defined in various ways. Typical of development economics is the notion of a labor force partly engaged in work having only marginal economic significance because of the nature of the activity and the low productivity of underemployed workers. (48) Applied to nations with large poverty populations, underemployment generally refers to servile occupations considered unnecessary in modernized circumstances, and which serve the purpose of social control by providing the poor with survival wages. Also implied are the ineffective use of human resources and the very limited labor capacity of workers who have little or no education and are chronically malnourished. In the present instance, some of these considerations are appropriate, but a different definition of underemployment is used for the following quantitative analysis.

By "underemployment" is meant less than a full year's work (50-52 weeks) and/or part-time work—less than 35 hours a week. Included are work patterns characterized by seasonal or episodic employment and jobs limited to a fraction of the regular time period of worker engagement. Routine jobs in the tourism and recreation industries exemplify seasonal activities, and sequential stretches of work with intermediate unemployment are illustrated by a house painter's helper, whose work depends on calls of varying length and complexity. Some jobs are steady but are performed on a fixed part-time basis only; say, 20 hours weekly as an office worker. In manufacturing, employment often depends on production rates, varying from full-time during the peak periods, to part-time when there is a slack, and to layoffs and unemployment following the curtailment of operations. These types of situations are distinguished for analytic purposes; but in actuality, a worker can experience any or all of the limitations mentioned.

The number of weeks or hours worked provides only a crude measure of underemployment and little or no information about the diversity of worker experience. Official data sources are generally limited to this kind of measurement, and whatever can be derived from the charteristics of workers reporting less than full-year, full-time employment. The SIE added several detailed questions to the basic time measurements, such as the reasons for part-year or part-time work and why a person was not in the labor force. In contrast with data already presented, retrospective comparisons were limited by a lack of information on this subject for Puerto Ricans in 1970 and 1960, and only a few comparisons with the total United States population were possible, owing to the fragmentary publication of the SIE information.

The full extent of underemployment remains, in any case, a matter requiring informed guesses and speculation. Lower-than-average labor force participation and higher-than-average unemployment are symptoms of underemployment, in that persons identified as neither working nor actively seeking work may be in an "off" season and those recorded as looking for work may be temporarily out of work in a series of job stretches. Further evidence of underemployment among Puerto Ricans derives from the occupational and industrial analysis already presented and qualitative information sources, which repeatedly refer to a lack of steady work as a typical situation.

Returning to the definition of underemployment in development economics, one discovers a certain resemblance between the work performed by Puerto Ricans in the United States and the condition of workers in third world nations. At least some of the jobs are servile and/or marginally productive—the type of employment eliminated or curtailed when capital-intensive reforms rely on mechanization, automation, or simply a more efficient mode of operation. The survival wages earned in underemployment keep Puerto Ricans from massive unemployment, which would threaten the maintenance of order and perhaps create a loud demand for drastic changes. In addition, it is plainly evident that human resources are underutilized and the psychic and bodily consequences of poverty are negative for the productivity of Puerto Rican workers.

THE PRECEDING YEAR

In answer to the question, "Last year, did this person work at all, even for a few days?" most men and about half of the women in the United States replied yes in 1970. As shown in greater detail in Table 22, a smaller proportion of Puerto Ricans had worked during the year preceding the Census, a difference reminiscent of the gap in labor force participation at the time of enumeration. Consistent with other results, the gap was particularly large in the teenage and young adult categories and among women of all ages. Comparing 1969 with 1975 data for Puerto Rican men, a decline was found in most age categories. This reduced the proportion for all ages to less than three-quarters, a very low figure by any standard, but especially indicative of unemployment in a relatively young population. Teenage and young adult women showed a higher percentage working in 1975 than in 1969, but even the higher levels were considerably lower than the measure for the total U.S. female population. An increase in American women's employment took place during the six-year period, involving a larger proportion working among those older than 35 years. (49) In this instance, a large difference was evident in comparison with Puerto Rican women of the same age, who had a decline of eight percentage points. Expectations based on general social change patterns would have mature women involved in work in greater number. The Puerto Rican exception to this pattern implied a lower percentage working for all women, which poses theoretical questions difficult to answer in research. (50)

22. PERCENT OF PERSONS WORKING DURING THE YEAR PRECEDING A CENSUS OR SURVEY, FOR THE TOTAL UNITED STATES POPULATION IN 1969; PUERTO RICANS IN 1969 AND 1975, BY GENDER AND AGE.

	PERCENT WORKING DURING THE PRECEDING YEAR*				
Age:	14-64	14-19	20-24	25-35	35-64
MEN:					
Total U.S., 1970	85.3	50.6	91.4	96.2	92.8
Puerto Ricans, 1970	80.0	31.3	82.5	89.4	85.4
Puerto Ricans, 1976	72.0	27.8	89.8	87.0	78.3
WOMEN:					
Total U.S., 1970	53.4	36.5	72.6	54.5	54.3
Puerto Ricans, 1970	38.1	23.9	49.0	34.1	37.5
Puerto Ricans, 1976	35.5	28.4	56.6	37.4	29.9

*Source: U.S. Census Bureau 1970 Census, Subject Report PC(2)-6A, Employment Status and Work Experience, and SIE Tabulations.

The conclusion that many Puerto Ricans are seriously underemployed is strengthened by information from the SIE regarding persons who had not worked during the preceding year. Claiming they had sought work were 23 percent of the men, and 10 percent of the women not working. This approximates the difference in measures of work during the preceding year between Puerto Ricans and the total U.S. population and points to serious problems in job placement. Seeking but not finding work also shows that the low level of labor force participation and high unemployment of Puerto Ricans is not a matter of voluntary choice in many cases. This became more apparent in the following breakdown of the measure considered, for teenagers and young adults:

percent seeking work	age:	14-16	17-19	20-22	23-25	26-28	29-31
among those not work-	men	(6)	(16)	42	34	35	39
ing in preceding year	women	(2)	20	19	12	11	(3)

With the exceptions noted in parenthesis, these figures were higher than those for Puerto Ricans age 14 to 64, indicating that underemployment was an even greater problem for young persons. Although it can be argued that labor force participation and employment are highest with persons in their early twenties, so too is the demand for jobs and the importance of starting a work career without a prolonged period of unemployment. The age sequence showed an abrupt change following the high school graduation stage (17-19) and relatively high percentages through the formative period of the work career, especially in the case of men. For Puerto Rican women, the percentages diminished as marriage, childbearing and related unpaid domestic activities became a more common alternative to seeking but not finding work outside the home. It must be noted in regard to these data that they represent a demand for employment additional to the unemployment typically measured in labor statistics. Persons seeking but not funding work for an entire year are likely to become discouraged workers, who eventually reduce their job seeking efforts and therefore may be classified as not in the labor force, when a survey is taken.

Another measure of underemployment resulted from responses to the question on the number of weeks worked, contingent on having worked during the year preceding the 1970 census and the SIE.

The figures presented in Table 23 show that in 1970 about two of every three men and two of every five women who had worked in the total United States population were employed during the entire preceding year. The difference between statistics for men and women makes clear that underemployment was much greater among women, many of whom worked on a short-time basis and experienced recurrent stretches of unemployment or labor force nonparticipation. A similar difference distinguished teenagers from older men and women; their typical work engagement was for a half year or less, many working during the summer vacation period, only. In the total United States population full-year work increased notably with age, for both men and women; by age 25 to 34 measures much higher than average were reached, suggesting that the process of settling into a work career was approaching completion in most cases.

Puerto Ricans differed from the general pattern in ways that are telling of the work of youth. As expected, proportionately fewer Puerto Ricans had a full year of employment preceding the SIE. This was not generally true of teenagers and young adults, however. In this instance, there was a greater tendency toward full-time work than in the total population. This indicates an earlier and more definitive entry to the labor force than usual in the United States, where many young adults continue schooling and work on a part-year basis until their mid-twenties. It also suggests that Puerto Ricans who actually find work as teenagers and young adults tend to work for longer stretches than average. The same contrast seemed to describe the situation of Puerto Rican women 25 to 34 years of age. Recalling the low labor force participation and high unemployment rates of this group, a higher-than-average measure of full-year employment seems reasonable for the fortunate few who sought work and actually found it. Perhaps the most important aspect is the condition of workers older than 35 years, who compensate for the relatively high rates of full-year employment among youth with much lower rates than average for the United States. Thus, instead of building up to steady work as a continuing pattern in maturity, working on full-year basis diminishes in frequency as Puerto Ricans advance in work careers.

23. PERCENT OF WORKERS BY WEEKS WORKED, FOR THE TOTAL UNITED STATES POPULATION IN 1969, PUERTO RICANS IN 1969 AND 1975, BY GENDER AND AGE.

	PERCENT OF WORKERS BY WEEKS WORKED		
	26 or less	27-49	50-52
TOTAL POPULATION, 1969			
MEN, AGE:			
14-64	13.2	19.5	67.3
14-19	62.4	21.4	16.2
20-24	23.5	26.8	49.7
25-34	4.3	18.8	76.9
PUERTO RICANS, 1969			
MEN, AGE:			
14-64	11.5	27.0	61.5
14 19	53.0	25.9	21.1
20-24	15.4	28.8	55.8
25-34	5.1	27.0	67.9
PUERTO RICANS, 1975			
MEN, AGE:			
14-64	14.9	23.6	61.5
14-19	78.5	9.3	12.2
20-24	12.1	35.2	52.7
25-34	17.5	20.5	62.0
TOTAL POPULATION, 1969			
WOMEN, AGE:			
14-64	28.9	27.8	43.3
14-19	67.4	20.6	12.0
20-24	34.4	29.9	35.7
25-34	28.6	29.5	41.9
PUERTO RICANS, 1969			
WOMEN, AGE:			
14-64	25.3	33.0	41.7
14-19	58.9	24.3	16.8
20-24	26.1	32.1	41.8
25-34	22.8	33.6	43.6
PUERTO RICANS, 1975			
WOMEN, AGE:			
14-64	27.2	28.4	44.4
14-19	56.7	17.7	25.6
20-24	37.7	27.7	34.6
25.34	22.2	18.3	59.5

SEASONAL WORKERS

If persons seeking work do not find at least short-time jobs, they are likely to eventually stop looking and cease to be defined in official statistics as available for work. The "discouraged" worker condition also affects Puerto Ricans because many experience an ongoing sequence of stretches of employment and unemployment, resulting in diminished work commitment as years of job insecurity run their course. Seasonal engagement is a characteristic of jobs performed by many Puerto Ricans. Assembly work, packing and wrapping, stock handling and incidential types of factory work depend on the production rate of manufactured articles. Helpers in gardening and restaurants, amusement center attendants and recreation leaders are typically hired temporarily as the annual cycle creates a demand for workers. Social action projects are often short-term or subject to budget changes and uncertainty about funding sources. Puerto Ricans in an "off" stretch when a census or survey is conducted may be recorded as not in the labor force or unemployed, depending on whether they are looking for work. Instead, they may be recorded as employed "with a job but not at work," a category abbreviated to "without work" in the following analysis.

Table 24 shows that in the total United States population the percentage of workers in this situation has slightly increased since 1960, a trend related to expansion in the number recorded as on leave for vacation. Other reasons for being without work have proportionately declined, including illness, bad weather, labor disputes and being "laid-off" or temporarily dropped from the payroll with expectations of returning to work. In comparison, Puerto Ricans had a somewhat higher rate of being without work in 1976, the only date for which such data were readily available. The difference in reasons was more significant; relatively fewer Puerto Ricans were on leave for vacation or illness and a much larger percentage were laid-off. A small proportion was recorded as taking time off for seeking another job, suggesting dissatisfaction or uncertainty with current employment.

Being a worker without work was more common for Puerto Rican women than men, and the rate generally increased with age—which coincides with other indicators of relative disadvantage in the labor market. In addition, Table 25 shows that both women and men who were workers without work in 1976 typically had only one job stretch

24. STATISTICS REGARDING WORKERS WITHOUT WORK, FOR THE TOTAL UNITED STATES POPULATION 1960, 1970, 1976 AND PUERTO RICANS, 1976.

	Total United States			Puerto Ricans		
	1960	1970	1976	1976		
Employed Workers: Percent					By Age and	
"with a job but not at work"	4.8	5.9	6.1	7.1	Gender, below	
Percent of Workers						
Without Work by Reason:						
Vacation	48.8	50.3	58.1			
Illness	29.2	28.5	25.4 } 83.5	62.7		
Bad Weather	5.2	2.8	1.4	0.0		
Labor Dispute	1.2	3.4	1.5	3.9		
Other	15.6	15.0	13.6	33.4	22.3	Laid Off
					3.1	Seeking Work
					8.0	Other

Puerto Ricans: Percent Workers Without Work

Age	14-19	20-24	25.34	14.64
Men	0.0	5.9	4.3	6.3
Women	7.2	4.4	12.9	8.4

*Source: U.S. Census Bureau, Statistical Abstract, 1976:363

25. INDICATORS FOR PUERTO RICANS EMPLOYED PART-YEAR, 1975-76

	MEN					WOMEN				
	14 & Older	14-19	20-25	26-31	32-64	14 & Older	14-19	20-25	26-31	32-64
EMPLOYED PART-YEAR	100	100	100	100	100	100	100	100	100	100
A. percent with										
one job stretch	80	80	78	76	82	80	100	61	100	75
B. percent spending										
rest of time:										
in school	50	93	63	9	7	28	80	25	5	0
in family care	3	0	0	25	4	48	4	59	91	61
with illness	19	0	9	3	47	18	11	4	4	34
other	28	7	28	63	42	6	5	12	0	5

during the preceding year. The question on how they spent the off time produced additional details. Among the responses most frequently checked, men specified enrollment in school more often than women; and women typically referred to involvement in family care. The contrast was particularly striking among workers 20 to 25 years old, implying that going back to school was a career option more open to men than women. Certain Puerto Rican women resumed their education during their early twenties, as previously noted. But they were relatively few in number. Traditional gender roles in the care of children and older persons thus seem to lessen chances for occupational improvement for young Puerto Rican women. This limitation continued for women age 26 to 31, who were predominantly engaged in family care when out of work. The SIE sample contained no cases of women age 32 and older who worked on a part-year basis and spent the rest of the time enrolled in educational programs.

Another important difference was apparent in the "other" category, which included employment in the armed forces, retirement and various specified responses which were combined into a single residual code in the SIE public use tapes. The undefined residual accounted for the second most frequent use of time among Puerto Rican men who were in a seasonal off period, and the leading category for those 26 to 31 years of age. This points to problems in the method of asking for information and a significant gap in knowledge about the situation of part-year workers. A similar difficulty affected data on illness, which was frequently mentioned by older men and women. No clear pattern emerged from the SIE data as to the temporary or continuing nature and severity of physical disabilities. Among all Puerto Ricans age 18 to 64 about one in five claimed a health condition limited the kind or amount of work possible. Most of the disabled (64 percent) stated that they could not work at all, an apparently high level of serious handicaps. However, when asked to identify their disability in a list of 14 conditions, about twice as many disabled persons checked "none of these," compared with the most frequently specified condition, respiratory disorders. The remaining categories were led by arthritis, rheumatism, back and spinal disorders—ahead of audiovisual impairments, heart trouble and mental, nervous and digestive disorders. These results show that a question composed for the total United States population left an information gap for Puerto Ricans, and that certain conditions experienced by many Puerto Ricans—anemia, malnutrition, infections, dental deficiencies, diabetes, schistosomiasis and other parasites, drug and alcohol dependency, cirrhosis of the liver and the consequences of accidents—should be specified among physical disabilities. (51)

PART-TIME WORKERS

Questionnaire problems also weakened the information gathered in the SIE regarding why many part-time workers did not have full-time employment. Among the reasons listed, "too busy" and "other" were checked by almost 40 percent of part-time workers, leaving a gap in our knowledge, since these are vague and un-defined responses. An additional 28 percent stated that their job was part-time in nature or that they could obtain only part-time employment—responses which indicate "structural" disadvan-tages in the job market. Reasons of a voluntary type, principally vacation and "does not want full-time work," accounted for only 18 percent; and illness, 14 percent. Again, a more detailed set of responses or a provision for coding the answers included in the "other" category would have provided more meaningful data for Puerto Ricans. In this and other instances where multiple code en-tries relate to a relatively small segment of a population, there is an additional problem of sample size. To obtain a valid and mean-ingful analysis sufficient cases are need for determining genuine differences between one category and another.

Related aspects of part-time work for which information was gathered in the SIE are summarized in Table 26. In general, these figures show that part-time work was more common for women than men and that both groups generally did not have a part-time job on a full-year basis, suggesting alternate time patterns such as stretches of full- and part-time employment, or short-term stretches of only part-time work. In either case the link between seasonal jobs and less than full-time engagement confirms the marginal labor market situation of many Puerto Ricans.

In so far as the number of cases in the SIE tapes permitted, the information for youth was tabulated in three-year age intervals, to portray differences that reflect employment changes occurring in the sequence from early teenage years to mature adulthood. For Puerto Rican men part-time work diminished sharply after age 19, but increased somewhat in the 32-64 category—following an

26. INDICATORS FOR PUERTO RICANS WORKING PART-TIME, 1975-76

	AGE							
	14 & Older	14-16	17-19	20-22	23-25	26-28	29-31	32-64
MEN								
EMPLOYED IN 1976:	100	100	100	100	100	100	100	100
Percent working part-time	14	76	36	19	6	11	5	13
EMPLOYED ONE YEAR BEFORE SURVEY	100	100	100	100	100	100	100	100
Percent working some part-time	22	86	66	29	23	12	20	16
Percent working part-time all year	11	11		5		2		15
WOMEN								
EMPLOYED IN 1976:	100	100	100	100	100	100	100	100
Percent working part-time	31	100	52	23	11	37	17	31
EMPLOYED ONE YEAR BEFORE SURVEY	100	100	100	100	100	100	100	100
Percent working some part-time	35	79	56	10	33	32	10	40
Percent working part-time all year	15	22		19		2		13

expected change pattern from summertime jobs to full-time placement and eventual time reductions as job security and employability lessened with age. In contrast, Puerto Rican women experienced only a moderate decline in part-time work following the teenage years and returned to a relatively high level after age 30. Among all ages, about one third of women working in 1976 had a part-time job, and among those working during the preceding year, half had part-time work on a temporary or yearly basis. Considered in relation to the greater number of women than men in the U. S. Puerto Rican population, the increased responsibility for households and the depressed labor force participation rates of Puerto Rican women, these data are very telling of why poverty continues and shows no sign of abatement.

FINDING JOBS

Merely calling for greater efforts to employ Puerto Rican women hardly provides an effective solution to a problem resulting from factors requiring significant social changes. Even the most ambitious program to find jobs in nondomestic work might leave untouched such barriers as community expectations of duty in family care, discrimination stemming from the belief that breadwinners are typically men, and negative strerotypes of women as less qualified, reliable and job-oriented. Recognition of domestic activities as work demanding payment, income maintenance without stigma, satisfactory arrangements for child care, effecutual help in coping with housing and credit biases—all represent policy directions for realistically dealing with the deprivation experienced by Puerto Ricans in the United States. Moreover, finding a job in itself does not necessarily mean economic improvement if future employment remains uncertain, pay levels continue below the cost of an adequate living standard, and promotion chances do not exist.

Data sources such as the SIE cannot be used to prove the need for the basic social changes just recommended, except as aggregate factual information points to human situations scarcely researched and discussed in the literature on Puerto Ricans. Whatever knowledge is available on how Puerto Ricans seek and find jobs remains a matter of assumptions drawn from the experience of other groups and conjectures based on distant and momentary observations. The figures in Table 27 present only a fragment of the information needed, among other reasons because the data were recorded only for persons who were unemployed at the time of the Survey. Therefore, no comparative information is available for persons who have a job, and the discouraged workers. Whatever can be derived from the SIE data about job procurement serves the purpose of improving the design of future research.

First regarding the reasons why Puerto Ricans were jobless and seeking work in 1976, we find that leaving school accounted for a relatively small percentage, except among men age 20 to 25. For teenagers, this may provide evidence of only a meager connec-

27. INDICATORS FOR PUERTO RICANS UNEMPLOYED, 1975-76

AGE	MEN					WOMEN				
	14 & Older	14-19	20-25	26-31	32-64	14 & Older	14-19	20-25	26-31	32-64
UNEMPLOYED IN 1976:	100	100	100	100	100	100	100	100	100	100
A. percent jobless and seeking work because:										
– left school	21	31	49	0	0	8	24	0	0	0
– lost job	48	1	43	92	75	36	0	41	83	44
– temporary job ended	14	42	0	0	2	24	41	17	17	14
– other reasons	17	26	8	8	23	32	35	42	0	42
B. percent seeking full-time job	85	62	100	100	99	82	56	93	83	99
C. percent seeking work by (1-4 non-exclusive means):										
1. public agency	49	41	62	56	46	36	40	35	34	36
2. applying to employer	34	48	63	19	14	41	52	57	19	31
3. advertisement	16	14	0	48	9	27	26	47	25	15
4. friends, relatives	27	28	16	41	23	13	12	5	25	12
5. none of these	24	8	23	34	28	15	23	8	8	24
D. percent by time spent seeking:										
1 month or less	30	56	36	10	15	35	54	25	20	33
1-6 months	35	37	20	50	34	49	46	54	43	53
6-12 months	17	6	30	16	22	5	0	0	19	7
year or more	18	1	14	24	29	10	0	21	18	7

tion between schooling and the job market, a pattern discussed in the literature on the educational situation of Puerto Ricans. (52) Considering that most teenagers have temporary and/or part-time jobs and may need continued employment during the school year, the combined percentages stating "lost job" and "job ended" seem reasonably higher than the proportions referring to leaving school. As in previous instances, the categories specified in the SIE questionnaire provided partial coverage of the reasons for unemployment. Only 4 percent stated that they had quit a job; the remainder of the "other" category represents reasons coded as "wants job for now," or simply "other." The residual was especially prominent among women, perhaps because many were returning to the non-domestic labor force following a stretch of household work, or discouragement about not finding a job—categories not specified in the questionnaire.

Both men and women showed a decided preference for full-time employment—a sadly inauspicious intention, compared with the statistics on the part-year and part-time jobs actually performed by most Puerto Rican workers. Responses to the question on means used to find work showed that for most of the jobless, the search involved more than intention. Typical of all gender and age groups was the use of more than one approach to the job market, as shown by the percentages exceeding 100 in total, due to separate calculation by frequency of the means mentioned. Application through a governmental agency was specified by nearly half of the men and more than a third of women seeking work, a seemingly high rate of utilization of public employment agencies, perhaps resulting from requirements for claiming unemployment compensation and public assistance, and the customary practice of applying for work at the Commonwealth of Puerto Rico's placement service.

The next most frequent means of finding work was by applying directly to potential employers, typically involving completion of the personnel forms in widespread use in commercial and service organizations. This approach was much more common among teenagers and young adults than older workers; in fact it surpassed the percentage using government agencies among applicants 14 to 25 years of age. Placing or responding to advertisements was frequent only among workers in their mid-twenties to early thirties. For older workers (especially men) reliance on friends and relatives was common, a pattern related to family and town-of-origin networks of information and influence that were described as a principal factor in migration from Puerto Rico and job placement some twenty to thirty years ago. (53)

The residual category "none of these" suggests that some persons seeking work (about one in five) did not use the established means of finding jobs in the United States or simply intended to look but did not take the steps for effective procurement. This orientation was more frequent among men and older workers, in general, and could be said by other writers to indicate a lack of effort to find employment. A different interpretation based on experience with Puerto Rican workers would argue that repeated instances of unemployment and rejection undermines the faith of certain persons in the established means of finding work, a process of discouragement leading others to stop looking for work, at all. Employment programs must therefore go beyond mere availability of placement services to provide a labor market reorientation sensitive to the consequences of chronic failure and despondency. The need for outreach and help in approaching an unfriendly environment applies also to workers who use an established means of finding a job. Although most workers used two of the established means, the average for older persons was a single approach to the job market and certain age/gender groups made minimal use of such practices as responding to advertisements.

Arguments blaming Puerto Ricans for not finding work find little or no supporting evidence in the data on length of unemployment. Most of the individuals recorded as jobless in the SIE had been seeking work for at least one month, typically for a few to several months (Table 27). In comparison, a somewhat shorter length of unemployment was true of the total United States population, in which close to 40 percent of the unemployed had been without work for less than a month, and 60 percent were jobless for two months or less. (54) Prolonged unemployment was particularly evident among workers older than 25 years, which accords with other information presented, but does not necessarily mean that younger workers had an easier time in finding work. The combination of high rates of nonattendance in school and low rates of labor force participation suggests that many Puerto Rican teenagers and young adults who could be considered as wanting work were not included among the unemployed. A broader definition of work intention would likely alter the Survey results to show a lengthy period of uncertainty involving wishes to have a job, despite alienation from schooling and conventional means of finding employment.

POTENTIAL EMPLOYMENT

The SIE produced some valuable information on persons recorded as not in the labor force and those not working during the preceding year, as summarized in Table 28. The most important finding is that about 40 percent of men and 26 percent of women classified as not actively seeking work answered "yes" or "maybe" when asked if they wanted a regular job. In addition to the unemployment data just discussed, this shows a considerable potential for economic activity that was not measured by the standard labor force question. The discrepancy between desire for work and attempts to find a job were particularly evident among persons age 20 to 29, whose potential for employment was two-thirds for men and one-third for women. The 42 percent of teenage women in this situation also represents a significant measure of hidden work intentions.

When asked why they were not looking for a job, many men who were potential workers replied that they thought that no employment was available for them, especially those older than 20 years and beyond the life stage when attending school provides a motive for not seeking work. This kind of discouragement was mentioned by a quarter of the teenagers not in the labor force, although attending school was their principal reason for not looking for a job. Family care was mentioned by about a quarter of the teenage women, showing that some had begun raising children or had responsibility for younger family members at home.

Women older than 20 years predominantly mentioned family care as the reason for not looking for a job, a category checked by only one percent of men out of the labor force. Of the family care responses, about one in five specified that not having child care available was the main labor force limitation. Both discouragement and domestic responsibilities are social factors not readily changed by existing labor programs, which assume that applicants envision a job resulting from their involvement and are at liberty to receive training and placement without major adjustments in their personal lives. Unless attempts are made to deal with such factors, the high employment potential of young Puerto Ricans will likely remain inactive.

Further evidence for observations made in this Chapter was provided by the data for persons not working during the preceding year, most of whom were not actively seeking work at the time of the SIE. More than a third of young adult males had sought but not found

28. INDICATORS OF EMPLOYMENT POTENTIAL FOR PUERTO RICANS, 1976.

AGE:	14 & older	14-19	20-24	25-29	30-34	35-64
MEN						
NOT IN LABOR FORCE:	100	100	100	100	100	100
A. Do you want a regular job? percent replying:						
yes	27	26	42	31	47	21
maybe	13	9	27	25	29	12
B. Why aren't you seeking work? percent:						
attending school	31	66	20	0		0
no work available	33	26	80	56		6
handicap or ill	30	0	0	44		68
NOT WORKING LAST YEAR:	100	100	100	100	100	100
A. percent sought work	19	9	33	35	39	25
B. Why not working? percent:						
attending school	49	90	69	0	1	0
could not find work	16	5	17	37	61	23
handicap or ill	32	3	4	61	38	74
WOMEN						
NOT IN LABOR FORCE:	100	100	100	100	100	100
A. Do you want a regular job? percent replying:						
yes	17	23	18	21	21	11
no	9	19	5	17	9	3
B. Why aren't you seeking work? percent:						
attending school	15	39	15	13		0
no work available	15	25	10	22		6
handicap or ill	13	3	0	0		34
family care	47	22	62	62		49
NOT WORKING LAST YEAR:	100	100	100	100	100	100
A. percent sought work	9	10	13	10	8	9
B. Why not working? percent:						
attending school	19	79	11	3	4	0
could not find work	6	4	4	4	9	6
handicap or ill	14	5	5	3	5	29
family care	59	8	75	90	81	64

a job and said that not finding work was the main reason for their inactivity—a circular reasoning indicative of discouragement and need for an improved life environment. Self-confidence and initiative cannot be reasonably expected of persons receiving little or no encouragement in this direction and often reminded of their unwanted position in society. It is also reasonable to suppose that many young women did not work nor seek work because of pressure to remain at home, expectations for family care, or the absence of an alternate reward system encouraging a career outside the home. Again, these are social factors which must be considered in the formation of public policy, if a genuine improvement in employment opportunities is the desired goal.

The possibility of returning to school was the subject of a question directed to persons age 18 to 25 not currently enrolled in formal instruction. In all, 53 percent of the men and 55 percent of the women said that they would like to return to school, and the proportions increased to 67 and 66 percent among those unemployed or having part-time or seasonal jobs, and were 62 and 48 percent among those not in the labor force. In an environment offering limited chances of finding work, this desire for schooling is no surprise. Some observers of training programs would further state that going back to school is a way of passing time and avoiding the inevitable reality of a jobless condition. But the percentages are high enough to also suppose that some of the Puerto Rican youth are genuinely concerned with the need for further schooling. The negative attitude toward schooling which accompanies the desire to leave before graduation may change as a result of a subsequent period of difficulty in finding employment.

Whether continued education contributes to work stability and occupational mobility will be discussed in the following Chapter. For reasons to be presented in detail, increased schooling does not offer an effective solution for unemployment and only a limited advantage in securing a more desirable job. The few exceptions are in employment sectors demanding postsecondary technical training, beyond the reach of many Puerto Ricans. Unemployment, underemployment and potential labor force participation thus remain largely without a remedy, except as the social environment could be altered to lessen the disadvantages of being Puerto Rican, and economic opportunities could be opened for effective placement and advancement in work careers.

SUMMARY AND SUGGESTIONS

Almost every aspect of employment among Puerto Ricans compared unfavorably with measures for the total United States population. The Puerto Rican unemployment rate was twice as high as the national average, and showed no sign of declining in the 1970s. But even this was a partial indication of job insecurity and the lack of employment opportunities. The unemployment rate did not include many persons who had sought but not found employment and eventually gave up looking for a job. For this and other reasons, Puerto Rican participation in the labor force was below average for the United States and showed symptoms of underemployment. By this is meant an unfulfilled potential for economic activity, expressed in such measures as:

- *a substantial percentage of persons outside the labor force who said that they would work, if they had the chance;*
- *the fact that most seasonal workers had only a single job stretch during an entire year;*
- *the small percentage of part-time workers who worked throughout the year;*
- *a longer-than-average period of unemployment;*
- *a high percentage of the jobless workers who gave termination from a temporary job as the reason for their unemployment.*

The picture emerging from the statistics is that of a population with very limited chances for full-time, full-year employment, and a very marginal condition in the engagement of the workers who are actually employed.

Puerto Rican teenagers were especially affected by the situation described. Many who left high school before graduation did not find jobs, or if they did, the employment was short-term and for limited hours. A significant proportion of teenagers were neither enrolled in school nor classified as in the labor force, presumably including persons who were discouraged from continuing a search for jobs, or for whom entry to the job market was a disconcerting and alienating experience. Thus, the transition to adulthood was marked by spells of inactivity for which conventional data sources have little or no explanation.

Responses to questions regarding the use of time and latent intentions to work indicated that most of the inactive teenagers would work if they had the chance. In fact, many eventually changed, away from the orientation to school described in Chapter

2, toward a desire for education as a means to obtain employment. However, considering the types of jobs performed by those who are employed (described in Chapter 3) little or no alternative existed to low-paid, low-mobility and insecure positions, except continued unemployment or inactivity. The data source in this study gave minimal coverage to nonconventional forms of work generally called "hustling," and sometimes related to the underground economy in Puerto Rican neighborhoods. Such activities as running errands, babysitting and helping people move may provide small amounts of money and early work experience. (55) But detailed research is much needed for going beyond these conjectures to a more valid portrayal of reality.

A decided change in the employment pattern was found among young adult men. In this case, labor force participation and the percentage of the employed having full-time jobs were high, providing a unique case of parity with the same age and gender group in the total United States population. However, the greater incidence of college and advanced schooling in the larger society must be considered as a factor in lessening the total population's work commitment among young men. In addition, the other employment indicators remained unfavorable for Puerto Ricans; for example, the unemployment rate was well above average, fewer workers had been employed during the preceding year, and so forth. The conclusion to be reached is that Puerto Rican young men enter the labor force somewhat earlier than others in the United States and are more likely to have full-time jobs, if they obtain employment. In this regard, we recall from Chapter 1 that many migrants from Puerto Rico were in this age group, persons presumably interested in finding full-time, full-year employment.

Puerto Rican young women had a labor force participation rate much lower than average for the United States total population. This was part of a general pattern of lower participation rates among Puerto Rican women, different from national trends and requiring detailed attention. From the analysis presented here we know that participation rates among teenage and young adult women actually increased from 1970 to 1976, while the decline which was general among Puerto Rican women in the 1960s continued at ages above 30 years. Compared with Puerto Rican men of the same age, women 17 to 19 years old had a lower school attendance rate and a higher participation rate. An abrupt change took place, however, for women in their twenties: expansion in labor force participation stopped at a level far below the equivalent measure for Puerto Rican men, and also below the level for women in the total population.

In 1976 unemployment severely affected Puerto Rican young adult women—at a higher rate than Puerto Rican men, and more than twice the rate for American women of the same age. Compared again with all women of the same age, a much smaller percentage of Puerto Rican women had worked during the year preceding the SIE, and were employed at the time the Survey was taken. Although direct evidence is not available from the SIE, it seems reasonable to assume that a formidable lack of employment opportunities was the principal explanation for the curtailed level of economic activity. Also, the demand for jobs was heightened by the large volume of migrants from Puerto Rico; no other age/gender group had as many recent arrivals as women aged 20 to 25. If these considerations are valid, the double disadvantage of being Puerto Rican and a woman provides a convincing reason why expectations based on the labor experience of other groups were not verified.

Other researchers using the same data base have analyzed the low level of economic activity among Puerto Rican women, from the viewpoint of labor markets and the social and economic characteristics of the population studied. (56) The findings show that Puerto Rican women's labor force participation increases with a higher local demand by employers for low-skilled female labor. Since this demand is very low in areas where Puerto Ricans live in large numbers, a lack of jobs explained the limited participation. Also on an aggregate basis, areas that have relatively attractive welfare payments are marked with low rates of women's economic activity, which the researchers view as related in turn to high rates of sole responsibility for households, particularly among women born in Puerto Rico. Except for the last aspect, which will be discussed in the following Chapter, these results confirm the observation made above; namely, that severe limitations in regional labor markets explain low participation rates. Other results add further evidence, mainly the relative job advantages afforded by education, English language proficiency and nativity in the United States. Under such highly competitive and restrictive circumstances, Puerto Rican young women born and schooled in the United States through the postsecondary level were found to be more often economically active and employed than other segments of the female population. To the extent that these social characteristics were not found, young women would be dissuaded by the un-promising outlook on the labor market, from seeking some sort of employment.

For Puerto Rican men and women older than age 30, employ-ment conditions were even less advantageous than for young adults. Presumably this had an influence on youth employment in that the lack of job opportunities and long-term (if not permanent) unemployment in the parent generation would seem to put pressure on teenagers and young adults to seek and maintain work. The data base used in this study provided only fragments of indirect evidence for this statement, which derives mainly from observation and experience in Puerto Rican communities. The sense of mutual dependence of people caught at the bottom of the United States social and economic structure may well be a major survival factor for Puerto Ricans of all ages. Perhaps the principal policy direc-tion emerging from the factual information in this Chapter is that Puerto Ricans must strengthen our responsibility for the wellbe-ing of others and our collective efforts to change and remedy a very negative condition.

Speaking in practical terms, how can this be done? Expanding on suggestions already made, the following seem workable:

1. We must develop networks of communication and mutual assistance, in which the extremely depressed economic condition of Puerto Ricans will be the subject of study and formation of strategies.

2. Teenagers and young adults must be included in these efforts, not just from the viewpoint of raising their awareness, but more importantly as a group who can actively contribute to solutions with their experience and ideas.

3. Specific issues must be raised in a collective way, so as to gain benefit from whatever resources are available outside the communi-ty. For example, the information presented on work disability showed that one-fifth of all Puerto Rican adults have a health condition that limits the chances of working. This and similar types of evidence can be used to pressure local authorities toward giv-ing some attention to the needs of the community.

4. Persons with knowledge and experience in the various aspects of employment should be identified and encouraged to assume an active role in the activities suggested. These persons should in turn involve others in the collective effort, with a view toward forming a Puerto Rican labor relations section as part of the agency pro-

posed in Chapter 3. This group would be prepared to analyze local job markets and seek openings in specific lines of activities that seem promising.

Again, as in earlier instances, these suggestions reflect a perceived need for community organization under circumstances in which public resources cannot be relied on to be operative in the case of Puerto Ricans. It is the author's considered opinion that Puerto Ricans must unite to cope with a situation that has eluded our control and for which we cannot expect solutions from the established system of economic and political organization.

5. TOWARD ANSWERING HOW

We recall from Chapter 2 that many Puerto Ricans continue in poverty or close to poverty, in ways resembling the situation of migrants from the island to the continent during the 1950s. A life pattern has emerged from that experience, which includes being the object of prejudice and discrimination in the types of jobs available or closed to Puerto Ricans. Exclusion from career opportunities leading to higher income and employment stability has left most Puerto Ricans trapped in a job market condition marked by low-paid, dead-end work; or simply unemployment. This has strengthened the population's dependence on transfer payments and has prompted people to develop survival strategies, exemplifed in the circular continent/island movement and the formation of households with more than one family or several earners, each receiving limited amounts in return for marginal economic activities of a part-time or seasonal nature. The social disorganization that accompanies long-term economic depression often has negative personal results, such as a lack of motivation to stay and succeed in school, leading teenagers to quit their education and seek the kind of work they perceive as what Puerto Ricans eventually do for a living, regardless of their degrees and qualifications.

A COORDINATED PICTURE

This Chapter aims at bringing together the various aspects of youth employment that have been analyzed separately, so as to add further evidence and detail to the statements just made, as well as to discover interrelations among the variables studied. Its purpose is to use a synthetic approach in answering questions of how the economic depression and deprivation affects Puerto Ricans.

The following multivariate analysis begins with evaluation of the income earned by Puerto Rican youth in relation to their employment situation and occupations. Later, these three variables become the subject of evaluation in terms of education and a variety of social and economic factors, such as migration, the language predominantly spoken and work disabilities.

Earned annual income ranged from zero to $18,500 for Puerto Ricans age 14 to 31 in the SIE data base. To relate this variable to employment, a work stability scale was composed by combining labor force status at the time of the SIE, labor force status one year before, and the length of time worked during the intervening period. The resulting measure ranged from zero for persons not in the labor force and not working during the entire period, to a value of five for those employed on a full-time, full-year basis. Trial cross tabulations of this scale with occupation, income and various social characteristic variables showed virtually identical results if the scale were condensed by combining scores one through four into a single category of part-time and seasonal work, along with cases of unemployment at one of the two points in time. The revised format was a three-point scale which had the following percent distribution of Puerto Ricans age 14 to 31:

	men	women
full-year unemployed or not in the labor force	28	56
partially employed	40	27
fully employed	32	17

This division had the advantage of providing sufficient cases in each category for further refinement by three six-year age groups: 14-19, 20-25, and 26-31. These categories are indicative of the sequence of life-cycle changes from the teenage period to establishment in work careers and served as a control variable in relating other variables to one another.

Based on considerations discussed in Chapter 3, the traditional occupational categories (professionals, managers, sales workers, etc.) were not used as a measure of the types of jobs performed by Puerto Rican youth. Variables devised from the complete listing of occupational titles proved to be awkward in relation to other variables, primarily because the limited number of cases in certain categories adversely affected the chances of obtaining valid results. Instead, the full occupational listing was used, as coded for prestige in the U.S. Commission on Civil Rights project regarding social indicators. (57) The prestige scores were drawn from recent surveys of people's evaluation of the relative social standing of jobs, which have been compared with objective criteria and found to reliably measure the desirability of different kinds of work. (58) The scale used here ranged from 1.5 for bootblacks to 88 for physicians. Scores for Puerto Ricans age 14 to 31 in the SIE sample varied from 5 to 74. The main advantages were to retain the diversity that would have been lost by combining occupational titles and to convert the job listing into a continuous variable for correlation with other variables, as a measure of the social worth attributed to the types of work performed by Puerto Rican youth.

The simple correlation matrix of income, employment and occupational prestige showed a high level of association in each pair of variables:

men	simple correlations	women
.683	employment and income	.734
.504	occupation and income	.561
.677	occupation and employment	.641

However, the separate importance of occupational prestige in relation to earned income was relatively small when the three variables were interrelated in multiple linear correlation. This result led to the composition of the following structure of influence of occupational prestige and employment on income:

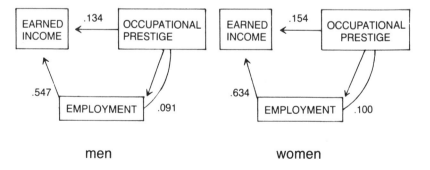

men   women

These diagrams show essentially the same pattern for men and women: employment explained earned income to a greater extent than job prestige—when the variation explained by each variable was statistically controlled, producing the standardized coefficients noted with the arrows showing influence. This suggested that occupational prestige and employment covaried in relation to income, as expressed by the curve without arrows in the diagrams. Calculation of path coefficients confirmed this interrelation and showed an indirect influence of occupational prestige on income, by reason of its influence on employment. The predicative strength of the model can be summarized as follows: the percent of the variation in earned income explained by employment and occupational prestige was 41.6 for men (40.7 and 0.9) and 55.2 for women (53.8 and 1.4).

These results show a generally matched condition between the kind of work performed by Puerto Rican youth and the income they received. The higher the social status of occupation, the more money was earned. *Nevertheless, having a job and working on a full-year, full-time basis was crucial to this matching of variables. This makes clear that employment itself is the most important factor in the economic situation of Puerto Rican youth.*

Certain aspects of the regression analysis provided additional information. The following summary statistics:

mean, earned income	
men	women
$3795	$1447

mean, occupational prestige	
men	women
21	20

showed that the money earned by Puerto Rican youth was much lower than the average $6047. for Puerto Ricans of all ages. Excluding persons without a coded occupation, the means of the prestige scores were also significantly lower than those for Puerto Ricans of all ages, which were found to be 32 for men and 33 for women in the U.S. Commission on Civil Rights study. (59) This is consistent with the pattern of involvement in low-paid, low mobility jobs illustrated by janitorial helpers, packers and wrappers, titles having prestige scores close to the mean for Puerto Rican youth.

Although men and women averaged about the same in job prestige, the income received by women was notably lower, indicating a differential in pay scales for similar types of work. In this analysis the length of time worked did not affect the comparison between occupation and income, because the time worked was statistically held constant. The scattergram of income and job prestige for women workers documented variation from a close linear relation in the range of prestige scores from about 23 to 48, involving many cases having lower incomes than expected on the basis of the general tendency and the corresponding scattergram for men. This level of job prestige is exemplified by sales clerks, general office help and skilled manual workers—occupations in which women face considerable disadvantages. These variations were not reflected in the correlation coefficient, which summarizes the general closeness of association between variables and does not measure the pattern of cases scattered around the line or curve of principal tendency.

From the beginning it must be stressed that the other variables used here were limited to attributes recorded in the SIE, which represent only a partial explanation for employment. If measures of individual social situations and such important factors as discrimination and alienation had been available, an analysis more sensitive to personal circumstances would have resulted. Research concerning Puerto Rican youth has also shown that structural features of life—such factors as differentials in opportunity, the political power of the Puerto Rican community, public policy and "chance" are as important for success as the demographic attributes recorded in the Census and similar questionnaires. (60)

When a social attribute (Spanish speaking) correlates with a condition (low school attainment) the link does not necessarily mean that the condition exists by reason of the attribute, nor that changing the attribute (learn English) will produce an improvement in the condition. Low school attainment may result from the school system's lack of concern for Puerto Rican students, especially those with language "problems." If school attainment is somewhat higher among English-speaking students, this does not automatically signify that they are receiving a better education, since their progress may be quite limited, in comparison with nonPuerto Rican students.

An assessment of social attributes is nevertheless worthwhile, because it aids in detecting symptoms to be considered in a general diagnosis of a problem. For example, a link between the use of Spanish and low school attainment could help in redirecting policy and teaching practice to be more responsive to the needs of Puerto Rican children, their cognitive style and career aspirations. It is especially important to avoid "blaming the victim" in the subject of youth employment, because the labor market has no responsibility for the employment of everyone wanting to work and of its very nature favors some, to the exclusion of to others. Labor improvement projects must cope with the disposition of employers seeking to maximize the return on their personnel costs, and in most instances cannot alter the social factors related to unemployment and underemployment. To illustrate, if the jobless tend to be inner-city residents, a placement program may envision facilitating transportation, but it usually cannot relocate potential workers nor eliminate negative attitudes toward applicants from a certain urban area.

EDUCATION AND EMPLOYMENT

The social factor most often related in the literature to the chances of finding a job and advancing in a work career are the years of educational instruction. Because of the limited number of cases in the SIE, the various levels of school attainment were condensed into four categories: less than high school; some high school; high school degree, and one or more years of postsecondary schooling. In order to retain age as a control variable, persons younger than age 20 who were currently enrolled were considered as high school graduates if their grade level showed attainment in the regular sequence. If the grade level of current enrollment showed a delay of at least two years "some high school" was considered the school attainment. This was based on previous research, which showed such a delay to be closely associated with noncompletion. (61) The attainment of teenagers not enrolled was taken to signify their level of completed schooling. The condensed and adjusted educational variable was then related to the variables earlier described, using the correlation method for men and women age 14 to 31.

The initial results showed that school attainment had a low to moderate degree of association with occupational prestige ($r = .224$ for men, .326 for women) but neglible to low correlations with earned income ($r = .149$ for men, .249 for women), and with employment ($r = .051$ for men, .251 for women). In order to test for a possibly strengthened association between education and the three variables considered together, the multiple regression method was used, with income as the dependent variable and no hierarchical ordering among employment, occupational prestige and education. The result was that education entered the equation after employment and occupational prestige and accounted for a negligible percent of the variation in income (men: 0.9, women: 0.2). The rest remained virtually the same as previously described. *This means that education added almost nothing to explain the economic condition of Puerto Rican youth, beyond what had been determined by employment and occupational prestige.*

The standardized correlation coefficients showed that when education was related to the other variables as a precondition, it had no direct association with earned income and was unrelated to employment. However, education retained a low degree of association with occupational prestige:

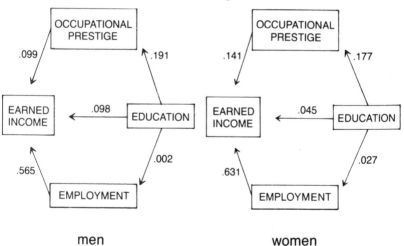

men   women

The path coefficients showed that the weak correlation between education and occupational prestige had an indirect influence on earned income. This slightly reduced the net influence of occupational prestige on earned income, showing that school attainment had played a minor role in economic wellbeing as it enabled certain workers to have somewhat more prestigious jobs. The much greater significance of employment remained unchanged for women and was slightly strengthened for men. *In other words, what really mattered in earning money was having a steady job, and if that happened, more schooling might signify a somewhat better posi-*

tion in social value. Except for the limited instances to be presently described, one's educational background made no difference in being employed, and had no direct bearing on how much money was earned.

The lack of association between employment and education was further examined for each age-gender group, as a test for latent influence and possible developmental changes from the teenage period to full establishment in work careers. In order to measure the latent influence of education, the social factors most closely associated with school attainment (later discussed) were combined into a single variable and entered with school attainment in a multiple regression on employment as the dependent variable. For education, the essential results were as follows:

	men, age:			women, age:		
	14-19	20-25	26-31	14-19	20-25	26-31
simple correlation with employment	– .096	– .204	.066	– .251	.385	.324
percent of variation in employment explained by education in multiple regression	0.8	4.1	0.4	6.3	2.7	0.7

These figures reveal certain aspects that modify the general pattern. For the groups showing a low negative association, education had a minor influence in not working, perhaps related to continued schooling--the only developmental pattern in evidence. In these cases multiple regression with other social variables (language, residential stability, marital status) showed that education accounted for a relatively small percentage of the variation in employment. For women older than 20 years, the moderate simple correlation with education also proved to be a residual factor in employment, when the influence of other social variables (household responsibilities, marriage, children, etc.) were statistically held constant. Thus, in no instance was there convincing evidence for a strong association between school attainment and employment.

The crosstabulations in Table 29 showed, however, that the lowest and highest categories of education had some influence on employment. Full employment was more frequent for both men and women with a technical school or some college education. For women, not being in the labor force was related to having left school before the secondary level; that is, with an elementary attainment.

In any case, the differences were not large, and the majority of Puerto Rican youth were concentrated in the "Some High School" and "High School Degree" categories, in which the variations were even smaller. The conclusion remains that the influence of education on employment was not strong.

29. PUERTO RICANS AGE 14-31 IN 1976: PERCENT DISTRIBUTION OF EDUCATIONAL LEVEL, BY EMPLOYMENT SITUATION

MEN	Total	Elementary	Some High School	High School Degree	Some Post-Secondary
not in labor force	100	7	33	52	8
partially employed	100	16	23	43	18
fully employed	100	12	31	30	27
all	100	12	28	41	19
WOMEN					
not in labor force	100	33	22	40	5
partially employed	100	22	16	46	16
fully employed	100	19	13	41	27
all	100	28	19	41	12

This general picture is consistent with the impressions held by many Puerto Ricans, which can be summarized in a lack of confidence in schooling as a path to economic improvements in the community. Schools are often viewed as a negative environment for Puerto Ricans, combining a failure to adapt to the needs of students with a lack of relation to the world in which the graduates will work and live. (62) Leaving school before graduation may actually make sense to some students, since this terminates the malaise and boredom fostered by the school environment, and agrees with the belief that continuation would not matter much in getting the jobs open to Puerto Ricans. From a statistical viewpoint, the fact that education is not strongly related to employment and means little for making money finds some explanation in the strong concentration of Puerto Rican youth in the partial high school and high school graduate categories. Jobs requiring these levels of schooling probably do not differ significantly in terms of prestige and income, when and where disadvantaged persons find employment. If a much larger proportion of Puerto Ricans completed college or advanced training in specialties having a demand in the job market, the relation between school and economic wellbeing might become positive. However, this remains largely speculative and open to the possibility of simply an upward shift in the education/employment disjunction, which has already happened. Today Puerto Rican youth generally have more education than the older generation had twenty years ago; and yet, the evidence shows no general improvement in their economic situation.

SOCIAL FACTORS

Many of the social attributes recorded in the SIE were interrelated among themselves. For example, Puerto Ricans who usually spoke Spanish also tended to be migrants, since those born in Puerto Rico are more likely to have this characteristic. To account for the association of variables, a comprehensive crosstabulation of social attributes was completed, using as many data items from the SIE as seemed appropriate for correlation with employment and education. For this purpose each nominal attribute was treated as a dichotomy; for example: veteran status, Spanish speaking, New York City residence and divorced status. The resulting values of one and zero were used for two-by-two contingency tabulations of use in eliminating redundant variables and tracing patterns of interrelation. (63)

To simplify presentation, the factors accounting for one percent or more of the variation in either employment or education are listed in Table 30, which provides an abbreviated matrix of measures of association with other variables. Generally speaking, the attributes that made some difference were characteristics reflecting the composition of the Puerto Rican community, health, marital status, and household living arrangements. The migrant variable was defined as having a birthplace differing from the State of current residence. As expected from Chapter 1, migration was negatively correlated with residence in New York City. This means that Puerto Ricans born outside their State of actual residence tended to live in places other than New York. Migrants also tended to use Spanish as their usual language. Although no additional pattern was apparent in regard to other social characteristics for Puerto Rican youth in general, certain attributes were associated with migrant status by age-gender group. For example, among teenage males, migrant status was associated with living in a household that supported an institutionalized or elderly person, and for men age 20 to 24 there was a similar correlation with the presence of children in a household.

Among teenage men and women the use of Spanish as a usual language was closely associated with being married or separated, and being responsible for the household in which they lived. This is consistent with the pattern of early marriage and household formation in Puerto Rico and may indicate cultural continuity. (64) For women older than 20 years, Spanish correlated with household responsibility, which meant that this status related also to migrant status because of the close connection between Spanish and migration. The association of these factors with the presence of children, residence in poverty areas and recent illnesses further indicated a link with disadvantages contributing to economic hardship. The composite picture leaves one with a discouraging impression of persons submerged in a condition of multiple problems and limited changes to improve their economic situation.

With minor exceptions, English as a usual language did not show an association with other variables, suggesting that Puerto Ricans who mainly speak English were evenly distributed among such categories as migrant and marital status. For men older than 20 years, however, English correlated with veteran status. This raises a question as to which variable influenced the other: did English-speaking persons have a greater tendency to be drafted and enlist, or did military service contribute to more frequent use of English? Another possibility is return migration to Puerto Rico among Spanish-speaking veterans, which in turn may be related to marital dissolution and the reduced number of young men in the U.S. Puerto Rican population. For teenagers and men age 20 to 25, veteran status was closely related to separation from their spouses and residence outside New York City, which is indicative of an uprooting experience for persons accustomed to early marriage and life in a strongly Puerto Rican environment.

The SIE variable on illness requiring medical attention during the preceding year proved important for the multivariate analysis, principally because in certain age-gender groups it was negatively related to employment and associated with such variables as Spanish language, which were negatively related to education.

30. PRINCIPAL CORRELATES OF FACTORS IN THE EDUCATION OR EMPLOYMENT OF PUERTO RICAN YOUTH, SELECTED IN APPROXIMATE ORDER OF EXPLANATORY IMPORTANCE.*

FACTORS IN EMPLOYMENT OR EDUCATION	CORRELATES, MEN					
	14-19		20-25		26-31	
MIGRANT	NYC	− .30	NYC	− .47	Separated	− .45
	Depend.	+ .25	Children	+ .33	NYC	− .42
	Spanish	+ .23	Cent city	− .32	Illness	− .40
SPANISH	Married	+ .19	Depend.	+ .33	Veteran	− .31
	Head	+ .18	Veteran	− .22	NYC	− .21
	NYC	+ .15	NYC	− .21	Disab.	+ .20
RECENT	Depend.	− .18	Disab.	+ .20	Disab.	+ .52
ILLNESS	Spanish	+ .14	Children	− .17	Separated	+ .51
	NYC	+ .11	Spanish	+ .15	Poverty	− .19
MARRIED	Cent city	− .15	Children	+ .26	Children	+ .63
	Migrant	+ .11	Depend.	− .23	Poverty	− .45
			Cent city	− .16	Disab.	− .28
OLDER	Poverty	− .26	Head	− .23	Disab.	+ .23
DEPENDENT(S)			Poverty	− .17	Head	− .15
			Migrant	+ .15	Spanish	− .15
VETERAN	Separated	+ .22	Separated	+ .31	Children	+ .23
	NYC	− .14	NYC	− .22	Married	+ .21
	Poverty	− .13	Migrant	+ .11	Cent city	− .11
NEW	Cent city	+ .47	Cent city	+ .42	Cent city	+ .59
YORK	Poverty	+ .41	Poverty	+ .33	Head	− .27
CITY			Children	− .19	Poverty	+ .26

*Simple bivariate correlations; redundant coefficients and those less than .10 were omitted. Abbreviations signify: Cent city: residence in central city; Depend.: support for institutionalized or elderly person(s); Disab.: work disability; Head: responsibility for household; Illness: sickness requiring medical attention during year preceding SIE; Migrant: someone

Table 30 *continued*

FACTORS IN EMPLOYMENT OR EDUCATION	CORRELATES, WOMEN					
	14-19		20-25		26-31	
MIGRANT	NYC	− .45	NYC	− .27	Spanish	+ .29
	Spanish	+ .43	Spanish	+ .22	NYC	− .15
	Cent city	− .13	Married	+ .13	Children	+ .14
SPANISH	Separated	+ .30	Head	+ .22	Poverty	+ .34
	NYC	− .28	Illness	+ .15	Head	+ .24
	Married	+ .28	Children	+ .14	Illness	+ .22
RECENT ILLNESS	Head	+ .35	Head	+ .38	Head	+ .51
	Poverty	+ .24	Children	+ .29	Poverty	+ .37
	Depend.	− .15	Poverty	+ .13	Disab.	+ .23
MARRIED	Poverty	− .26	Poverty	− .26	Poverty	− .27
	Cent city	− .16	Spanish	− .13	Depend.	− .21
	Migrant	+ .11	Depend.	− .11	Spanish	− .18
OLDER DEPENDENT(S)	Poverty	− .22	Cent city	− .21	Children	− .29
			Spanish	− .13	Separated	+ .26
			NYC	− .13	Spanish	− .11
HOUSEHOLD RESPONSIBILITY	Spanish	+ .17	Children	+ .41	Children	+ .34
			Disab.	+ .17	Poverty	+ .30
			Poverty	+ .16	Migrant	+ .11
NEW YORK CITY	Cent city	+ .28	Cent city	+ .55	Cent city	+ .40
	Poverty	+ .27	Disab.	− .11	Disab.	− .12
	Separated	− .12				

not born in the State of current residence; NYC: residence in New York City; Poverty: resident in a sample unit with 20 percent or more of all families having income below the poverty line; Spanish: use of Spanish: as the usual language.

Among women, recent illness was closely related with household responsibility and poverty, indicating an important link with economic distress. It should also be noted that recent illness did not correlate with work disability in some of the age-gender categories. This means that additional to the chronic health factors limiting economic activity, certain sicknesses debilitated Puerto Rican youth in their work and schooling. Moreover, the question on health insurance showed that only 78 percent had some sort of coverage for the payment of medical services. *Considered as a set of circumstances, these variables clearly showed that ill health was a major contributing factor to economic depression affecting the Puerto Rican community.*

A similar factor that requires more research is the support provided by Puerto Rican youth to elderly and institutionalized persons. A crude indicator for this variable was devised from household data on support for institutionalized persons, and the presence of persons older than 65 years, who generally showed almost no labor force participation and very limited or no income in preliminary crosstabulations. Like recent illness, "older dependents" showed a pattern of association with other social attributes accounting for education and employment. But "older dependents" was not as consistently related to the economic distress factors as recent illness. In some age-gender groups, it was negatively related to poverty and Spanish as a usual language, and a positive factor in education and employment. Technical limitations in relating personal attributes to household composition and the lack of background literature on the topic do not allow for making convincing generalizations beyond the fact that a general need to support older persons was in evidence, and that this provided both a stimulus and a limiting condition in regard to economic activity and schooling.

Residence in New York City was strongly associated with central-city locations and living in a "poverty area," defined as a geographic unit having 20 percent or more of the total population receiving family incomes below the poverty threshold. This did not mean that Puerto Ricans living outside New York escaped the realities of the ghetto. In other cities, Puerto Ricans tend to be somewhat more dispersed and may be impoverished without living in a geographic unit demarcated as a "poverty area." Where Puerto Ricans are clustered in a barrio, their share of the total population may still be limited, especially in the "buffer zones" between predominantly white and black areas, neighborhoods which are very heterogeneous in composition, if stable—or not currently described by the Census Bureau information as "poverty areas," if in transition. Moreover, the multivariate analysis showed the significant net influence of central-city or "poverty area" residence in regard to employment, regardless of residence in New York City.

The clustering of social variables generally confirmed assumptions previously proposed as an explanation for the economic situation of Puerto Rican youth. But more questions emerged than could be answered. At best, the wide range of social attributes recorded in the SIE explained about forty percent of the variation in employment and education, leaving a major portion to be studied in subsequent research. Although it is impossible to fully determine the unexplained variance, much would be clarified if additional information, different from government survey and Census data, were available. For example, we need to know how the family history and make-up of households influence in the schooling and work patterns of Puerto Rican youth. The types of schools attended, the kind of preparation for labor force entry and variations in cognitive and behavioral skills are all crucial to an understanding of how people approach careers and become involved in work situations. Again, the lack of knowledge about the process of seeking jobs, finding or not finding work, and the complexity of factors in the job market leave the structural elements of analyses largely unknown. These variables, as well as the broader issue of prejudice and discrimination, are factors that differ in a qualitative way from the characteristics of the population that have been analyzed in this study. Therefore, whatever connections can be made between the attributes of Puerto Ricans and the social and economic environment remain hypothetical and in need of examination in further research. Perhaps the most limiting deficiency is the lack of documentation of factors external to the Puerto Rican community that determine its educational and employment chances in the American system. Such information would likely reduce the unexplained variation to levels at which policy directions for the larger society would be relatively clear and predictions for Puerto Ricans could be made on a valid basis.

FACTORS IN EDUCATION

In order to identify the social attributes most closely associated with education, all of the characteristics used for the analysis just described were entered without hierarchical ordering in multiple correlation using the regression method. Only those factors accounting for one percent or more of the variation in education will be presented, along with the simple correlation coefficients, showing the degree of association without considering the other factors. Attributes not presented in Table 31 accounted for only a fraction of one percent of the variation in education for each age-gender group. This in itself represents an important result, because included among the nonexplanatory variables were such items as a physical disability or English as a usual language. More variables are presented than would seem necessary to account for the variation in education, so that the relative unimportance of certain items can be noted in conjunction with those most closely associated.

An overview of Table 31 reveals that several variables that appeared to be closely associated with school attainment in simple correlation turned out to be relatively minor sources of influence when all of the variables were considered in multiple correlation. Although most of the factors showed a negative relation to school attainment, this does not imply that unrelated characteristics had a positive influence. For example, Spanish as a usual language was the factor most commonly associated with school attainment, in a consistently negative way. But English was unrelated to education, failing to explain one or more percent of the variation in school attainment. *This means that Spanish speaking persons tended to have limited schooling, while English speaking persons were proportionately distributed from low to high in educational background.*

In some instances, the migrant factor, defined as anyone not born in the State of current residence, had some explanatory value, although less than Spanish as a usual language. In the case of teenage men, this meant that changing residence from one State to another (or Puerto Rico/continent) was negatively associated with school attainment. Among men and women age 20 to 25 an alternative pattern may have been limited school attainment as a factor in migration, if the movement took place after leaving school. *In either case it is clear that migration and educational advancement did not go together for Puerto Rican youth. Very importantly, this affected both Spanish and English speaking persons.* A lack of

31. PRINCIPAL VARIABLES CORRELATED WITH THE EDUCATIONAL ATTAINMENT OF PUERTO RICAN YOUTH, DERIVED FROM THE SURVEY OF INCOME AND EDUCATION, 1976.

Men	Simple Corre- lation	Percent of Variation Explained	Women	Simple Corre- lation	Percent of Variation Explained
Age 14-19 Variable			Age 14-19 Variable		
Spanish Speaking	−.37	13.6	Household head	−.44	19.1
Veteran	−.20	4.5	Married	−.32	12.7
Migrant	−.23	1.8	Spanish Speaking	−.33	2.6
Older Dependent(s)	+.09	1.0	New York City	+.19	1.2
New York City	−.02	1.0	Central City Area	−.03	1.6
(Multiple Correla- tion) and Total	(.48)	21.9	(Multiple Correla- tion) and Total	(.62)	37.2
Age: 20 – 25 Variable			Age: 20 – 25 Variable		
Spanish Speaking	−.42	17.8	Migrant	−.40	16.4
Migrant	−.37	8.5	Household Head	−.37	12.2
Older Dependent(s)	−.02	2.2	Married	−.01	4.0
Recent Illness	−.19	2.0	Spanish Speaking	−.35	4.1
Household head	−.16	1.2	Poverty Area	−.12	2.4
			Separated/Divorced	−.22	1.5
(Multiple Correla- tion) and Total	(.57)	31.7	(Multiple Correla- tion) and Total	(.64)	40.6
Age: 26-31 Variable			Age: 26-31 Variable		
Veteran	+.46	21.2	Recent Illness	−.40	15.9
Spanish Speaking	−.43	9.2	Spanish Speaking	−.36	7.5
Separated/Divorced	−.14	3.0	Children	−.28	4.5
Household Head	+.07	2.8	Older Dependent(s)	+.26	2.4
Older Dependent(s)	−.17	2.0	Migrant	−.29	2.3
New York City	−.04	2.5	New York City	+.12	1.3
(Multiple Correla- tion) and Total	(.64)	40.7	(Multiple Correla- tion) and Total	(.58)	33.9

school system adaptability in the United States and Puerto Rico probably accounts for the negative relation between migration and education. Such problems as differences in curriculum, improper placement of transfer students and a generally negative attitude toward the migrant were likely to contribute to poor performance and the "push out."

For teenage men, military service was negatively associated with school attainment, suggesting that persons who quit school enlist in the armed forces to a greater extent that those who continue in school. However, veteran status was positively related to school attainment among older men likely to have served in the late 1960s and early 1970s. Unfortunately, the data did not allow for an examination of the provocative question of whether this represents a developmental pattern (as Puerto Ricans engage in military service and advance in age, their school attainment improves) or whether the age differences reflect historical and generational patterns. Perhaps military service once contributed to educational improvement, but diminished in significance from about 1968.

For teenage and young adult women being married and/or assuming sole responsibility for a household was a major negative factor in educational attainment, to an even greater extent than speaking Spanish as a usual language. These variables disappeared as influences in education for women age 26 to 31, but in this group having children proved to be a limiting factor. However, on the basis of these data we cannot adequately distinguish between the consequential and developmental aspects of schooling and family formation. It could be argued that women with low school attainment tended to marry at younger ages and have a greater number of children. Alternatively, involvement in marriage and childbearing in a male-dominated society could be said to have restricted the chances for women to continue education. As in other instances in which the evidence cannot be stretched beyond its explanatory power, most likely both patterns were true to some degree, and probably interrelated. A more detailed explanation would require longitudinal or life history information.

FACTORS IN EMPLOYMENT

The social attributes accounting for employment either differed from those accounting for education, or correlated in a different way. As in the analysis of education, the percent of the variation explained by social attributes generally increased with age, ranging from only 16 percent for teenage women to almost half for men age 26 to 31. Again, a single characteristic or at most two accounted for most of the variation that could be explained on the basis of information from the SIE, indicating that many social attributes were redundant or added very little to the analysis. Only those factors accounting for one percent of the variation or more are presented in Table 32.

The factor most strongly associated with employment among teenage men and women proved to be marriage with spouse present. We recall that this variable was interrelated with migrant status and the use of Spanish as a usual language. It was unrelated to education for teenage men and a negative correlate for teenage women. These considerations suggest that the typical teenage full-time worker was from Puerto Rico, had quit school, married early and assumed responsibility for a household. However, the multiple correlation showed important modifications in this pattern. Among teenage women, employment was negatively associated with migrant status, indicating that those moving from Puerto Rico to the United States may not have sought or found work. A similar situation was in evidence regarding households supporting an institutionalized or elderly person; in these instances, teenage women tended to either not work or have part-time employment. A contrary indication among teenage men suggests greater reliance on young men as supplementary earners in cases of older dependents. For teenage men, English as a usual language proved to be an economic advantage, a unique instance in the analysis presented in this Chapter. English was unrelated to education and negatively associated with the migrant-Spanish-marriage and household responsibility set of variables. In view of these differences we suppose that English may have explained why certain Puerto Rican teenagers had full-time, yearly jobs while others had part-time or seasonal work. But precisely what influence it had could not be clearly determined, based on the analysis completed.

For other age-gender groups, language was not a significant factor in employment, or if present, was more effectively accounted for by

32. PRINCIPAL VARIABLES CORRELATED WITH THE EMPLOYMENT OF PUERTO RICAN YOUTH, DERIVED FROM THE SURVEY OF INCOME AND EDUCATION, 1976.

MEN	Simple Correlation	Percent of Variation Explained	WOMEN	Simple Correlation	Percent of Variation Explained
AGE 14-19 Variable			**AGE 14-19** Variable		
Married	+ .24	5.9	Married	+ .33	10.6
New York City	− .23	4.7	Migrant	− .13	2.8
English Speaking	+ .15	2.9	Older Dependent(s)	− .15	1.2
Poverty Area	+ .01	2.2	Recent Illness	− .19	1.5
Older Dependent(s)	+ .12	2.6	(Multiple Correlation) and Total	(.42)	16.1
Veteran	+ .16	2.5			
(Multiple Correlation) and Total	(.46)	20.8			
AGE 20-25 Variable			**AGE 20-25** Variable		
Recent Illness	− .42	17.4	Children	− .46	21.3
Married	+ .18	4.6	Recent Illness	− .38	7.0
Children	− .02	2.7	Migrant	− .22	3.1
Migrant	+ .08	2.1	New York City	− .17	4.3
Older Dependent(s)	− .21	2.2	Poverty Area	− .21	2.4
New York City	− .06	3.1	(Multiple Correlation) and Total	(.62)	38.1
(Multiple Correlation) and Total	(.57)	32.1			
AGE 26-31 Variable			**AGE 26-31** Variable		
Work Disability	− .60	35.4	Recent Illness	− .43	18.4
Central City Area	+ .37	5.9	Migrant	− .33	8.0
Separated/Divorced	− .17	4.1	Older Dependent(s)	+ .24	4.1
Poverty Area	− .15	2.0	New York City	+ .19	2.4
Veteran	+ .14	1.5	Children	− .27	2.2
Migrant	− .01	0.8	Work Disability	− .17	1.6
(Multiple Correlation) and Total	(.70)	49.7	(Multiple Correlation) and Total	(.61)	36.7

such variables as migrant status. This result must be considered in relation to prevailing explanations of the employment problems experienced by Puerto Ricans, which repeatedly identify limited English speaking proficiency as a negative factor in finding jobs and advancing in work careers. Our data show that certain other factors were much more important determinants of employment. *For example, illnesses and disabilities accounted for a major portion of the variation in employment among persons older than 20 years, suggesting that health conditions may require more attention in the improvement of employment opportunities than efforts to compensate for the linguistic identity of potential workers.* These results also suggest that the importance of language as a barrier to employment may be mediated by other characteristics, such as personal appearance, place of birth, schooling, place of residence or the means taken to seek work.

The lack of a relation between language and employment was clearly evident in the percentages of persons usually speaking Spanish:

	men	women
not in the labor force	25	50
partially employed	24	38
fully employed	22	50
total	24	47

These figures show a remarkable consistency among men, and a relative uniformity among women. An important difference is noted, however, in that Puerto Rican women had twice the tendency to speak Spanish, as a usual language, in comparison with men. This reflects the greater proportion of women who are migrants from Puerto Rico, and suggests that Spanish-speaking men have a greater tendency for return migration to Puerto Rico. Perhaps differences in exposure to English or willingness to identify Spanish as the usual language spoken account for some portion of the variation.

For women age 20 to 25 the presence of children in the household was a major negative factor in employment. Although this could be expected in an age group having many persons in the child-bearing and early child-rearing stages of the life cycle, it must be recalled that many young Puerto Rican women with children were solely responsible for the households in which they live. The lack of effective solutions for meeting the demands made by employment outside the home means that many women in this situation had little or no choice in staying home. It will be noted that all of the factors associated with employment for women age 20 to 25 were negatively correlated—having a recent illness, being a migrant, a resident of New York City or living in a poverty area—all were disadvantages, even when the relative influence of each of these was statistically held constant. Most Puerto Rican women are likely to have at least one of these attributes, and in contrast, no data item from the SIE was found to positively correlate with employment. On balance, the odds were clearly against having full-time yearly employment.

Essentially the same picture describes the economic situation of women age 26 to 31, with the exception that having older dependents and living in New York City were positively associated with employment. One gathers the impression that the transition to middle age and establishment in whatever work careers were possible involved a period of conflicting social expectations, marital changes, segmental labor force participation and eventual stabilization in a household responsibility role involving a long-term commitment to raising children in adverse economic circumstances. None of the marital status attributes correlated with employment for women older than 20 years, suggesting that it did not matter whether a person was married, separated, divorced or widowed. This is consistent with the interpretation just given and shows that in itself, being married with spouse present was not a factor keeping young Puerto Rican women from seeking work and being employed outside the home, beyond 25 years of age.

In contrast, being married with a spouse present correlated positively with employment among men age 20 to 25. Independent from this influence, the presence of children was a minor negative factor. In conjunction with the results for women in the same age category these tendencies suggest that among young Puerto Rican couples various combinations of work involvement existed—both spouses working part-time; one on a seasonal basis, the other unemployed, and so forth. It is also clear that the traditional division of work into "domestic: women" and "nondomestic: men" was not as sharp as could be expected on the basis of cultural background. Most likely the pattern of work involvement had more to do with the need to earn money and the chances to find a job. Faced with the high costs of household formation and child-rearing, many Puerto Rican couples probably considered themselves fortunate if either spouse could work on a full-time, yearly basis.

Among men age 26 to 31 separation or divorce was negatively associated with employment, to the extent that men involved in the dissolution of marriage had a greater tendency to be unemployed, or employed on a part- time or seasonal basis, than the currently married or single. Again, the precise character of the influence remains unclear. Did the maritial break-up result from chronic unemployment and low levels of earned income, was it the opposite way, or did both evolve together? Longitundinal and life history information might help clarify why so many Puerto Rican marriages end in separation or divorce. Early marriage may motivate early work involvement, with reduced chances for steady work and advancement; then, an economic crisis may develop as children are born and expenses increase, leading to separation and divorce. Alternatively, it could be argued that Puerto Ricans younger than age 26 to 1976 were influenced by a changed environment, favoring the postponement of marriage and innovation in male/female roles in work involvement and household responsibility.

It must be noted in regard to employment, as in the case of education, that more questions are raised by the analysis presented than can be answered from conventional data sources. Field studies, direct observation and collective interviews would provide information on variables that remain largely unknown, or matters for conjecture at present. From our research it is apparent that influences hardly touched in labor surveys have a direct and decisive bearing on whether Puerto Ricans find jobs and the types of work they perform. The SIE data make it clear that health, migration, place of residence, family life and household composition are more important than education and language, the factors most often cited as determinants of employment.

Beyond personal attributes, the social environment and labor market conditions, (for which we have only fragments of information) make up a major portion of the unaccounted variation. If these factors could be measured and integrated in the analysis, they would likely clarify the influence of personal attributes, as these could be analyzed in more detailed and meaningful ways. For example, among men age 26 to 31, employment was positively associated with central-city residence, but negatively associated with poverty—area residence. This result may reflect better mass transportation in such cities as New York, joined with a reluctance among employers to hire people with addresses in the South Bronx and East Harlem.

The development of effective labor policies does not have to await more research to begin now. Regardless of alternative explanations and statistical refinements, our research reveals the need for a strenuous effort by community agencies and the government to provide for the effective placement of Puerto Ricans in full-time, yearly jobs. It has also made clear that changes are needed in the school system and other organizations intended to help Puerto Rican youth in their careers. *Beyond opening opportunities in a job market that clearly disfavors Puerto Ricans, policy must be directed to consider such factors as ill health and nutritional problems, the disruption of frequent migration, family responsibilties and culturally defined expections not always typical of conventional society in the United States or Puerto Rico.* Although Puerto Ricans have been repeating this message for at least three decades, it has not found a receptive attitude among policy makers in the United States and Puerto Rico, nor had an effective influence on programs intended to improve labor conditions. Today, Puerto Rican youth are as disadvantaged as the older generation was in 1960.

EMPLOYMENT AND ECONOMIC CONDITIONS

A final comment on the relation between the employment of Puerto Rican youth and economic conditions among Puerto Ricans of all ages returns the discussion to the initial considerations regarding poverty and dependence on transfer payments. The combination of employment, job prestige and earned income previously described can be related to certain variables measuring the consequences of limited opportunities for Puerto Rican youth. In particular, depressed economic conditions for youth can be studied in relation to dependence on food stamps, aid to families with dependent children, other forms of public assistance, government subsidized housing, and unemployment compensation. In addition, the lack of bank accounts is indicative of low income and credit limitations; no health insurance is often a by-product of unemployment or partial employment, and having more than two earners and/or two or more families in a household are adaptive measures to cope with a very low level or the absence of earned income.

The conditions just mentioned were combined into a single index ranging from zero for Puerto Rican households having none of the consequent attributes, to ten if all were present. The tabulations of the SIE data presented in Table 33 show that no household had a score higher than six points. The mean score was 2.3 for households recorded as male-headed, 2.4 in those where women had sole responsibility. In view of this approximation and the relatively similar distribution pattern of scores, no major difference was evident between the two types of household responsibility. Both male- and female-headed households showed a very low percentage of zero scores; the typical situation was two or more conditions indicative of economic hardship. *These data serve to dispel the ideas that certain Puerto Rican households are well-off if the family's income rises above the poverty line, and that having a man as responsible would in itself improve a household's economic condition.* The evidence shows that regardless of who is the responsible person, Puerto Rican households were generally in a clearly disadvantaged situation, indicative of a multiplicity of negative influences from an environment keeping people in poverty or close to it.

33. PERCENT DISTRIBUTION OF HOUSEHOLDS WITH ONE OR MORE PUERTO RICANS AGE 14-31 IN 1976, BY SCORE ON A TEN POINT SCALE OF ECONOMIC HARDSHIP* AND ACCORDING TO THE EMPLOYMENT SITUATION OF YOUTH WHO WERE HOUSEHOLD MEMBERS.

YOUTH EMPLOYMENT	HOUSEHOLDS RECORDED AS HAVING A MAN RESPONSIBLE							
	0	1	2	3	4	5	6	Total
not in labor force	5	8	53	22	10	2	-	100
partially employed	3	14	33	28	13	9	-	100
fully employed	10	34	30	21	3	2	-	100
total	6	19	37	24	9	5	-	100

YOUTH EMPLOYMENT	HOUSEHOLDS HAVING A WOMAN WITH SOLE RESPONSIBILITY							
not in labor force	13	12	22	26	19	8	-	100
partially employed	2	18	38	25	10	6	1	100
fully employed	4	33	45	9	8	1	-	100
total	9	17	31	23	15	5	-	100

*Scale items adding one were: foodstamps, aid-to-dependent children and other welfare recipiency; unemployment compensation; government subsidized housing; below average rent or mortgage; no bank or saving account; no health insurance; two or more families in a household; and more than two earners.

In multiple correlation with the consequence scale, the combination of employment, job prestige and earned income produced coefficients of -.409 for male-headed households (with earned income as the principal factor) and -.298 where women were solely responsible (with employment as the principle factor). These results provided evidence of a moderate negative association between the economic condition of Puerto Rican youth and dependence on transfer payments and economic deprivation in the households in which they live. *In other words, as the employment, job prestige and income of youth improved, the various features indicative of poverty in Puerto Rican households diminished.*

These results tell us that the gainful employment of Puerto Rican youth provides an important solution to the economic depression that characterizes the Puerto Rican community, in general. Although it cannot be considered a panacea nor a substitute for efforts to employ older persons, the economic success of youth would have a decidedly positive influence on the future of all Puerto Ricans. In this book we have used factual information to present a picture of youth employment that leaves very much to be changed, if this positive consequence is desired. Repeated instances of negative measures of economic activity have led to a general conclusion that a substantial reform in the environment affecting Puerto Rican youth is necessary. Only by way of comprehensive measures to change the opportunity structure can some solution be found to underemployment, unemployment and a lack of correpondence between education and income production. In the author's opinion neither the United States government nor the government in Puerto Rico will likely move in the policy directions needed for such changes. The book therefore ends with an appeal to Puerto Ricans and whomever else is interested in our destiny to join networks of people who are actively engaged in efforts to solve the grevious problems with which we live.

FOOTNOTES

The following publications were repeatedly utilized in the preparation of the book. The titles have been abbreviated in the footnotes and illustrations as indicated below:

Original Form	Abbreviation
U.S. Bureau of the Census	U.S. Census Bureau
U.S. Census of Population: 1950 (U.S. Government Printing Office, Washington, D.C., 1953)	1950 Census
Vol. II, *Characteristics of the Population* Part 1. United States Summary	Characteristics: United States
Vol. IV, *Special Reports*, Part 3, Chapter D, Puerto Ricans in Continental United States	Report on Puerto Ricans
U.S. Census of Population: 1960 (U.S. Government Printing Office, Washington, D.C., 1961-1964)	1960 Census
Vol. I, *Characteristics of the Population* Part 1, United States Summary	Characteristics: United States
General Social and Economic Characteristics	Social and Economic Characteristics
Detailed Characteristics	Detailed Characteristics
Subject Reports. Final Report PC(2)-1D. *Puerto Ricans in the United States*	Report on Puerto Ricans
Historical Statistics of the United States, Colonial Times to 1957; Continuation to 1962 and Revisions, 1965.	Historical Statistics
Census of Population: 1970 Vol. I Characteristics, General Population to Detailed	1970 Census (as in 1960)
Subject Reports. Final Report PC(2)-1E. Puerto Ricans in the United States	(as in 1960)
Subject Reports. Final Report PC(2)-1C. Persons of Spanish Origin	Report on Spanish Origin
Current Population Reports P-20, No. 264, 267, 290, 302, 329, 339, 354. "Persons of Spanish Origin in the United States: March 1973-79."	CPS Spanish Origin Report(s) 1973-79
P-20, No. 334, "Demographic, Social and Economic Profile of States: Spring 1976."	SIE Report
Statistical Abstract of the United States: 1970-79	Statistical Abstract, 1970-79
Current Population Reports, Special Studies P-23, No. 82, "Coverage of the Hispanic Population of the United States in the 1970 Census, A Methodological Analysis, 1979."	1970 Census, Hispanic Coverage Report
U.S. Commission on Civil Rights	U.S. Civil Rights Commission
Social Indicators of Equality for Minorities and Women, 1978	Social Indicator Report
The following is an example of successive references:	
ASPIRA of America. Social Factors in Educational Attainment Among Puerto Ricans in U.S. Metropolitan Areas, 1970. New York, 1976.	ASPIRA. Social Factors.

1. For more details, see U.S. Census Bureau, Data Access Descriptions, No. 42: "Microdata From the Survey of Income and Education," 1978.
2. U.S. Census Bureau, 1970 Census, Hispanic Coverage Report:22-23, 30-35.
3. A detailed discussion of age categories in labor force research is presented in U. S. President's Science Advisory Committee Panel on Youth. Youth: Transition to Adulthood. Chicago: University of Chicago, 1972:9-29.
4. U.S. Census Bureau, 1970 Census. Report on Puerto Ricans. CPS. Spanish Origin Reports, 1973-78.
5. The 764,960 recorded in 1970 as self-identified Puerto Ricans who were neither foreign-born nor born in the United States are assumed to represent those born in Puerto Rico. The 810,087 reported as born in Puerto Rico include an undetermined number of persons who did not identify as Puerto Rican, presumably individuals of other ethnic origins represented in the United States population. U.S. Census Bureau, 1970 Census. Reports on Puerto Ricans and Spanish Origin. Our tabulations of the SIE showed that in 1976 persons born in Puerto Rico and self-identified as Puerto Rican were estimated at 812,253 or about 50,000 more than the 1970 Census figure. If the 50,000 increase is subtracted from the 111,230 estimated by the SIE to have migrated from Puerto Rico to the United States from 1970 to 1976, a rough estimate of 60,000 return migrants is obtained. This would signify a yearly average of 20,000 migrants from Puerto Rico and 10,000 returning from the United States, a net gain of some 10,000 persons from 1970-1976. These figures of net gain accord with increases in the Puerto Rican population, as measured in the Current Population Survey, when considered in conjunction with estimates of natural increases in the U.S. Puerto Rican population.
6. Variations in the publication format of household relation data make comparisons difficult on this topic. The 1978 figure is from U.S. Census Bureau, CPS. Spanish Origin Report, 1978:37, which provided data on female head of household for Puerto Rican families only, not for all Puerto Rican households. The last published information for both categories (Spanish Origin Report, 1975:36-37) showed female heads to be 36.5 percent for families, 38.1 for households— indicating a higher rate when

the more general definition is used.

7. Cuervo, Lilia. Matrimonio en Puerto Rico: estudio socio-demográfico, 1910-1968. Rio Piedras, P.R.: Editorial Edil, 1971. Also relevant to comparisons with this study are results from SIE tabulations on changes in marital status subsequent to first marriage. Contrary to expectations based on tradition, remarriage did not seem to be increasing among divorced women, who often face serious disadvantages as single parents and have been encouraged by Puerto Rican society to reenter a husband-wife relation. Consistent with this drift from tradition, the percentage remaining widows has decreased among older women, who were discouraged from remarriage in the past. Evidence for these suppositions was provided by responses to the SIE question on whether a person was married more than once. Unfortunately, this was asked only in cases where "now married or widowed" was the reported marital status, which eliminated possible analysis for persons currently divorced, separated or specifying "never married." The available information shows that only 7 percent of Puerto Rican women currently married had been previously married and divorced—lower than expected, considering the number currently divorced, and Puerto Rico's divorce rate. Former widows made up 5 percent of those currently married and more than a third of Puerto Rican women who reported ever being widowed. These proportions seem high, given the force of social customs and the advanced age typical of widowhood, and as in the case of divorce, provide evidence of factors contributing to increases in sole responsibility for households among women.

8. U.S. Census Bureau, 1960 Census. Report on Puerto Ricans:32, 56, 96. 1970 Census. Report on Spanish Origin:24. 1976, SIE tabulations.

9. For more details, see Cooney, Rosemary S. and Alice Colón. "Work and Family: The Recent Struggle of Puerto Rican Females," Pp. 58-73 in Clara E. Rodríguez and others. The Puerto Rican Struggle. New York: Puerto Rican Migration Research Consortium, 1980.

10. Carr, Norma. "The Hispanic Presence in Hawaii," and Camacho Souza, Blaise. "Hawaii's Puerto Ricans," Pp. 10-13, 36-37 in United Puerto Rican Association of Hawaii, Inc. Souvenir Program Book, Miss Latina-Hawaiiana Pageant, 1977.

11. An example of North Central birthplace and migration patterns is provided by Santiago, Anne A. "The Puerto Rican Community in Milwaukee: A Study of Geographic Mobility." M.A. Thesis in Geography, University of Wisconsin, Milwaukee, 1978.

12. U.S. Census Bureau, CPS, P-60:124, "Characteristics of the Population Below the Poverty Level: 1978" and "Technical Documentation of the 1976 Survey of Income and Education," by Paul T. Manka, 1977.

13. Self-employment income averaged at a mean of $258 and made up the largest portion of receipts for work other than salaries and wages and returns on wealth. However, among Puerto Rican workers, only four percent received self-employment income and about one third of these also received wages and salaries; generally their total incomes were high. Farm income, received by only one household in the sample, was an insignificant factor in the average for all households. Only sixteen percent of Puerto Rican households had income from dividends, interest, rentals and royalties, received mainly from money on deposit in savings accounts. Together, these sources accounted for about $140 of the mean total household income.

14. The criteria for eligibility and related information were drawn from U.S. Congress, House of Representatives. Hearings Before the Committee on Agriculture: Food Stamp Program, Investigation and Extension. Washington, D.C., 1973:21-22 and MacDonald, Maurice. Food Stamps and Income Maintenance. New York: Academic Press, 1974.

15. The SIE tabulations showed that 8 percent of Puerto Rican women having custody of children received alimony or support payments during the preceding year. This was low compared with published information from the SIE showing that 25.3 percent of all women having children (and not living with a spouse) received support payments. For women of Spanish origin, 16.5 percent was the corresponding statistic. U.S. Census Bureau, CPS. P-23:84, "Divorce, Child Custody and Child Support," 1979:13.

16. This view is based largely on comparisons with the experience of European ethnic groups, as in Fitzpatrick, Joseph P. Puerto Rican Americans: The Meaning of Migration to the Mainland. Englewood Cliffs, N.J.: Prentice-Hall, 1971:1-9, 130-154. In addition to the analogy with immigrant groups, this source places

importance on participation by the Puerto Rican community in the improvement of public education and portrays prospects for advancement in an essentially optimistic way.

17. Examples of this viewpoint include: Wachtel, Howard M. "Capitalism and Poverty in America." American Economic Review 62 (May 1972):187-194. Carnoy, Martin (ed.) Schooling in a Corporate Society: The Political Economy of Education in America. Second Edition. New York: McKay, 1975. Bowles, Samuel and Herbert Gintis. Schooling in Capitalist America: Educational Reform and Contradictions of Economic Life. New York: Basic Books, 1976.

18. ASPIRA. Social Factors: 1-7.

19. ASPIRA. Social Factors. The CPS Spanish Origin Report for 1979:25 provided essentially the same information as presented in Table 13. For example, among Puerto Ricans aged 20-24 and 25-29, about 45 percent had not completed high school, 20 percent had some post- secondary instruction, but only 6 percent were college graduates.

20. ASPIRA. Social Factors:15. In certain metropolitan areas, social promotion policies have led to the use of pregraduation achievement tests to certify students for receiving a high school diploma. Students obtaining scores below a certain level receive only certificates of attendance.

21. Socialization to limited educational and occupational horizons has been found among blacks living in conditions similar to those of Puerto Ricans. Rist, Ray C., The Urban School: A Factory for Failure. Cambridge: MIT, 1973. It is therefore argued that the aspiration levels of high school students accord with the racial limitations in the job market. Jenks, Christopher and others. Inequality: A Reassessment of the Effect of Family and School in America. New York: Harper, 1972.

22. An overview of the development policies of the Commonwealth of Puerto Rico and their implications for unemployment and underemployment is provided by Frank Bonilla and Ricardo Campos, "A Wealth of the Poor: Puerto Ricans in the New Economic Order," Daedalus, Spring 1981: 133- 176. The argument presented leads to the conclusion that emphasis on a capital-intensive model has created a labor surplus, originally involving agricultural workers, but now affecting the secondary and tertiary sectors, as well.

23. The principal proponent of the "culture of poverty" perspec-

tive was, of course, Oscar Lewis, "The Culture of Poverty." Scientific American, 215:19-25, and La Vida. New York: Vintage, 1968. It is widely ignored, however, that notions of "cultural deprivation" and "blaming the victim" were essential elements of U.S. government policy toward Puerto Ricans during the social program era inspired by the Kennedy-Johnson administrations.

24. Statements of the conventional human resource model are very numerous. One of the few that are sensitized to issues discussed here is Lester, Richard. Manpower Planning in a Free Society. Princeton, N.J.: Princeton University. 1966.

25. An unusually insightful study of human resource development in partially closed societies is Curle, Adam. Educational Strategy for Developing Societies. London: Tavistock, 1963.

26. Gernes, Arthur C. "Implications of Puerto Rican Migration to the Continent Outside New York City," New York: Migration Division, Department of Labor, Commonwealth of Puerto Rico, 1955.

27. New York State Department of Labor. Characteristics of Population and Labor Force, New York State, 1956 and 1957. Vol. V, Puerto Ricans (white and non-white) in New York City. June, 1961.

28. The decline in operative jobs is discussed in Wagenheim, Kal. A Survey of Puerto Ricans on the U.S. Mainland in the 1970s. New York: Praeger, 1975: 67-70 and Centro de Estudios Puertorriqueños, History Task Force, Labor Migration Under Capitalism: the Puerto Rican Experience. New York: Monthly Review, 1979:117-177.

29. The school system has been called a "channeling colony" in that caste and exploitation in employment influence educational policies regarding discriminated groups in the United States; for example, a study of Mexican Americans in Santa Clara County found a higher return rate for schooling among workers not completing a certificate level, since jobs were more typically open to "dropouts" than to graduates. A similar difference was found between rural and urban workers in Puerto Rico, suggesting a hierarchy of exclusion in economic participation, which left most migrants to the United States unprepared for the American job market. Carnoy, Schooling in a Corporate Society: 93. A more general study of the topic is provided by Spring, Joel H. The Sorting Machine: National Educational

Policy Since 1945. New York: David McKay, 1976.

30. For example, young Puerto Ricans were portrayed as hospital attendants in the film, "All That Jazz." An apparently widespread practice in bilingual programs is to employ an English-speaking teacher having some academic background in Spanish as the instructor, with a native speaker of Spanish as a teacher's aide. The status difference in authority and prestige is considerable, and justified on the basis of seniority, certification and experience in teaching. For this reason the education and placement of Puerto Ricans as bilingual instructors were stressed by the National Puerto Rican Task Force on Educational Policy. Toward a Language Policy for Puerto Ricans in the United States: An Agenda for a Community in Movement. New York, 1978:33-35, 40-41.

31. U.S. Census Bureau. Statistical Abstract, 1977:411.

32. In most recorded cases of manual work in 1975 there was less than a dollar difference in minimum hourly wages between the figure for advanced levels (for example, journeymen and truck drivers) and pay for helpers and laborers. U.S. Census Bureau, Statistical Abstract 1979:417. A general description of factory/white—collar differences in career development and the narrowing of wage differences between skilled and nonskilled workers is provided by Cohen, Sanford, Labor in the United States, Fifth Edition. Columbus, Ohio: Charles E. Merrill, 1979:253-279.

33. U.S. Census Bureau, Statistical Abstract, 1977:411, 451-2.

34. Public Opinion (June/July 1982): 34, also quoted in Diálogo, Quarterly Newsletter of the National Puerto Rican Policy Network (Fall 1982):3.

35. Pifer, Alice. "Wanted: Employment Agencies that Don't Discriminate." Perspectives (Fall/Winter 1981) Vol. 12, No. 3:16-23.

36. Rodríguez, Clara. The Ethnic Queue in the U.S.: the Case of Puerto Ricans. San Francisco: R & E Research Associates, 1973.

37. U.S. Census Bureau. Technical Paper No. 38, "Comparison of Persons of Spanish Surname and Persons of Spanish Origin in the United States," 1975.

38. Among other sources, New York Times National Recruitment Survey, October 12, 1980. The downward squeeze on the job market has resulted from a very complex set of factors, in-

cluding the 1946-64 "baby boom;" the overproduction of high-level resources by the educational system; the displacement of workers by mechanization, automation, computerization, and the failure of public policy to adequately address the employment needs of young Americans.

39. U.S. Census Bureau. CPS, SIE Report:118.

40. The labor force participation of Puerto Rican women is compared with that of other Hispanic groups in Newman, Morris J., "A Profile of Hispanics in the U.S. Work Force," Monthly Labor Review, December 1978:3-14.

41. The high unemployment rates of minority youth in 1975 are discussed in U.S. Congress, Joint Economic Committee, Youth and Minority Unemployment, Washington, D.C., July 6, 1977:1-13. Factors involved in first-job procurement and hiring are analyzed in Ornstein, Michael D., Entry into the American Labor Force. New York: Academic Press, 1976. National Commission for Manpower Policy. From School to Work: Improvement in the Transition. Washington, D.C., 1976.

42. In 1970 about 60 percent of Puerto Rican youth were leaving the educational system before high school graduation, which is consistent with the data presented for 1976 if men and women are combined. ASPIRA Social Factors:16,42.

43. The concept and measurement of "discouraged" worker unemployment are discussed in the Monthly Labor Review 96,3 (March 1973):8-37. 97,9(September, 1974):28-30. 101,9 (September, 1978):15-25, and 101,10 (October, 1978):40-42.

44. An overview of national unemployment is provided by Cohen, Labor in the United States:413-431.

45. The lack of information on Puerto Rican unemployment and related statistcal problems are discussed in U.S. Civil Rights Commission. Improving Hispanic Unemployment Data: The Department of Labor's Continuing Obligation. Washington, D.C.

46. U.S. Census Bureau. Historical Statistics and Statistical Abstract, 1977:355.

47. U.S. Civil Rights Commission. Social Indicator Report:32.

48. For example: Meier, Gerald M., Leading Issues in Economic Development. Studies in International Poverty, Second Edition. London: Oxford University:149-158.

49. U.S. Department of Labor. Women and Work, R&D Monograph 46, Washington, D.C., 1977:13-18.

50. Newman, "A Profile," and Cooney, Rosemary Santana and Alice E. Colón Warren, "Declining Female Participation among Puerto Rican New Yorkers: A Comparison with Native White Nonspanish New Yorkers Ethnicity," 1976, 6:281-297.
51. Alers, José Oscar and others. Puerto Ricans and Health: Findings from New York City. New York: Fordham University Hispanic Research Center, 1978 1-29 and 79-84.
52. For example, Fitzpatrick, Puerto Rican Americans, 1971:130-154. Canino, María, "The New York Public School System and the Puerto Rican," Pp. 101-105 in A New Look at the Puerto Ricans and Their Society. New York: Brooklyn College Institute of Puerto Rican Studies, 1972.
53. At the height of the migration from Puerto Rico, a reporter wrote: "Nearly every newcomer is met at the plane by relatives or friends (who) will usually take him in to live. The next thing is to find a job... One of them will take the new man to his factory... If that doesn't succeed, he'll try something else." Rand, Christopher, "A Reporter at Large - The Puerto Ricans, Part III, Among the Cold People," The New Yorker (December 14, 1957):87. According to Handlin, Oscar, The Newcomers. New York:Anchor, 1962:71-72, about the only possibility of upward mobility for Puerto Ricans in the 1950s were jobs that "dealt with members of their own group... (especially by) opening groceries, meat markets, bodegas and other little shops that catered to the distinctive tastes of their fellows."
54. U.S. Census Bureau. Statistical Abstract:395.
55. For blacks, this kind of work is described in Valentine, Bettylou. Hustling and Other Hard Work. Life Styles in the Ghetto. New York: Free Press, 1978.
56. Cooney, Rosemary Santana, "Intercity Variations in Puerto Rican Female Participation," Journal of Human Resources, 1979, 14:222-235, and Cooney, Rosemary Santana and Vilma Ortiz, "Hispanic Female Participation in the Labor Force: A Comparative Analysis of Puerto Ricans, Mexicans and Cubans," paper presented at the Population Association of America annual meeting, 1981.
57. U.S. Civil Rights Commission. Social Indicators: 34-38.
58. Temme, Lloyd V., Occupation: Meanings and Measures. Washington, D.C.: Bureau of Social Science Research, 1975.
59. U.S. Civil Rights Commission. Social Indiciators: 36.
60. ASPIRA. Social Factors: 30-44.

61. ASPIRA. Social Factors: 15-23.
62. National Puerto Rican Task Force. Toward a Language Policy: 1-15 and Civil Rights Digest, Vol. 6, No. 2, Special Issue: Puerto Ricans in the Promised Land: 21-28.
63. The regression method with dichotomous variables is described in Nie, Norman H., SPSS Statistical Package for the Social Sciences, Second edition. New York: McGraw-Hill, 1975:222-230, 373-383.
64. Cuervo, Matrimonio en Puerto Rico: 36-40.

INDEX

ABOUT THE AUTHOR

José Hernández was born in Jersey City, N.J. His mother was Blanca Alvarez, a school teacher from Utuado, who served as an assistant to the Commissioner of Education of Puerto Rico, and then studied at Columbia University Teachers College—the original reason for migration to the United States. His father, José Hernández, who is from Puerta de Tierra, San Juan, graduated from the University of Pennsylvania in Philadelphia, and after some thirty years of dental practice and community activities in the New York area, returned to Puerto Rico, where he lives with the author's stepmother, Carmen Esteva, in Santurce.

Like many other Puerto Ricans of the "Marine Tiger and Novela Palmolíve" generation, the author enjoyed listening to Mayor Laguardia read the funnies to the children of New York on Sunday mornings. He attended P.S. 17 and St. Francis Xavier High School in Manhattan, and Fordham University in the Bronx. He liked social studies, writing, photography and running track. After two years as a high school teacher in Puerto Rico, he studied for a Ph.D. in sociology at the University of Minnesota, specializing in labor economics and human resource development.

Next, Hernández worked for a year at the Social Science Research Center, University of Puerto Rico, and then as a research sociologist at the International Population and Urban Research Center, University of California—Berkeley. Out of this experience came his first book, *Return Migration to Puerto Rico,* 1967. As a program advisor to the Ford Foundation, the author lived in Brazil and traveled widely in Latin America and Asia. This provided the insight for *People, Power & Policy,* a book which deals with poverty and population growth in third world nations.

As an associate professor at the University of Arizona and guest lecturer at several college campuses in the West, Hernández became acquainted with the concerns of Chicano and American Indian youth in the early 1970s. During this time he co-authored *Cuantos Somos: A Demographic Study of the Mexican Americans.* Later he was employed by the U.S. Commission on Civil Rights to organize the project that eventually produced *Social Indicators of Equality for Minorities and Women.* While in Washington, D.C. he participated in the politics leading to enactment in 1976 of U.S. Public Law 94-311, which made mandatory the identification of Spanish origin persons in federal data collection forms. He also served as chair of the Hispanic advisory committee for the 1980 Census.

Returning to academics, Hernández taught introductory sociology to thousands of students in mass lectures at the University of Wisconsin—Milwaukee. He also taught minority studies and research methods at the graduate level. He was a founder and president of the Puerto Rican Migration Research Consortium, a professional association of social scientists. In addition to this book, Hernández has contributed to various publications on Puerto Rican topics, such as *The Puerto Rican Struggle: Essays on Survival in the U.S.* and "Social Factors in Educational Attainment Among Puerto Ricans," published by ASPIRA of America.

Recently, the author moved to Chicago, where he served as an advisor in research to the Hispanic Alliance at De Paul and Loyola Universities and Mundelein College. For most of 1983 he was research director of the Latino Institute, in charge of data analysis and publication efforts. At the time *Puerto Rican Youth Employment* was published, the author was preparing to begin work as a professor in the Department of Black and Puerto Rican Studies, Hunter College, City University of New York.